ALL MOD CONS

by Erica Murray

samuelfrench.co.uk

THINKING ABOUT PERFORMING A SHOW?

There are thousands of plays and musicals available to perform from Samuel French right now, and applying for a licence is easier and more affordable than you might think

From classic plays to brand new musicals, from monologues to epic dramas, there are shows for everyone.

Plays and musicals are protected by copyright law, so if you want to perform them, the first thing you'll need is a licence. This simple process helps support the playwright by ensuring they get paid for their work and means that you'll have the documents you need to stage the show in public.

Not all our shows are available to perform all the time, so it's important to check and apply for a licence before you start rehearsals or commit to doing the show.

LEARN MORE & FIND THOUSANDS OF SHOWS

Browse our full range of plays and musicals, and find out more about how to license a show

www.samuelfrench.co.uk/perform

Talk to the friendly experts in our Licensing team for advice on choosing a show and help with licensing

plays@samuelfrench.co.uk   020 7387 9373

Acting Editions

BORN TO PERFORM

Playscripts designed from the ground up to work the way you do in rehearsal, performance and study

---

Larger, clearer text for easier reading

Wider margins for notes

Performance features such as character and props lists, sound and lighting cues, and more

---

+ CHOOSE A SIZE AND STYLE TO SUIT YOU

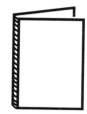

STANDARD EDITION

Our regular paperback book at our regular size

SPIRAL-BOUND EDITION

The same size as the Standard Edition, but with a sturdy, easy-to-fold, easy-to-hold spiral-bound spine

LARGE EDITION

A4 size and spiral bound, with larger text and a blank page for notes opposite every page of text – perfect for technical and directing use

---

LEARN MORE | **samuelfrench.co.uk/actingeditions**

Other plays by ERICA MURRAY
published and licensed by Samuel French

The Cat's Mother

FIND PERFECT PLAYS TO PERFORM AT
www.samuelfrench.co.uk/perform

MUSIC USE NOTE

Licensees are solely responsible for obtaining formal written permission from copyright owners to use copyrighted music in the performance of this play and are strongly cautioned to do so. If no such permission is obtained by the licensee, then the licensee must use only original music that the licensee owns and controls. Licensees are solely responsible and liable for all music clearances and shall indemnify the copyright owners of the play(s) and their licensing agent, Samuel French, against any costs, expenses, losses and liabilities arising from the use of music by licensees. Please contact the appropriate music licensing authority in your territory for the rights to any incidental music.

IMPORTANT BILLING AND CREDIT REQUIREMENTS

If you have obtained performance rights to this title, please refer to your licensing agreement for important billing and credit requirements.

ABOUT THE AUTHOR

Erica is originally from County Limerick, Ireland. She holds an MFA in Playwriting from the Lir Academy, Trinity College Dublin. She was a member of the Soho Young Writer's Group and the New Playwrights Programme at the Lyric Theatre, Belfast, where she developed *All Mod Cons*. This year she is one of the recipients of the Channel Four Playwrights Scheme bursary award supported by The Peggy Ramsay Foundation. Her first play, *The Cat's Mother*, was long-listed for the Verity Bargate Award, it premiered in 2018 and toured to Underbelly at the Edinburgh Fringe and the Dublin Fringe Festival, where it won the Fishamble Award for Best New Writing.

DIALOGUE

/ means the next line of dialogue overlaps here.

—means an interruption or an unfinished thought.

"Mam" is a colloquial Irish term, please change as suits the production.

SETTINGS

A fictional city.

Most of the action takes place in **JEAN** and **GARY**'s mother's house; 98 Linton Avenue, and numerous average properties that are for sale.

The set should be non-naturalistic so the play can change between places easily.

ALL MOD CONS

All Mod Cons premiered in Belfast on 22 May at the Lyric Theatre in the Naughton Studio.

CAST (IN ALPHABETICAL ORDER)

JEAN	**MARIAH LOUCA**
IAN	**CHRIS McCURRY**
LAURA	**SOPHIE ROBINSON**
GARY	**MICHAEL SHEA**

CREATIVES

WRITER	**ERICA MURRAY**
DIRECTOR	**RONAN PHELAN**
SET AND COSTUME DESIGN	**DIANA ENNIS**
COMPOSER & SOUND DESIGN	**KATIE RICHARDSON**
LIGHTING DESIGN	**SARAH JANE SHIELS**
DIALECT COACH	**BRENDAN GUNN**
EXECUTIVE PRODUCER	**JIMMY FAY**
PRODUCER	**BRONAGH McFEELY**
CASTING DIRECTOR	**CLARE GAULT**
PRODUCTION MANAGER	**ADRIAN MULLAN**
COMPANY STAGE MANAGER	**AIMEE YATES**
DEPUTY STAGE MANAGER	**SIOBHÁN BARBOUR**
ASSISTANT STAGE MANAGERS	**STEPHEN DIX**
	KERRI McGIMPSEY
	SOPHIE THOMPSON
COSTUME SUPERVISOR	**GILLIAN LENNOX**
COSTUME ASSISTANT	**ERIN CHARTERIS**
SENIOR TECHNICIAN	**IAN VENNARD**
TECHNICIANS	**ADRIAN WALL**
	CORENTIN WEST
	TIGHEARNAN O'NEILL
FIGHT DIRECTOR	**IAN McCRACKEN**

CAST

MARIAH LOUCA
JEAN

Mariah Louca recently graduated from Guildford School of Acting. Her previous credits include: *The Interview* (The Biscuit Factory) and *Julius Caesar, Playing for Time, A Dream, The Sheffield Mysteries, 20 Tiny Plays About Sheffield* (Crucible Theatre). She will appear in the upcoming short film *Re-Displacement* (Rural Media/ The Sheditors) opposite BAFTA-nominated Nico Mirallegro released in 2019.

All Mod Cons is Mariah's professional debut since graduating GSA.

CHRIS McCURRY
IAN

Chris was born in Belfast and currently lives in London. He was a member of the Lyric Drama Studio in 2012 and is a graduate of the Royal Welsh College of Music and Drama. Previous Lyric Theatre credits include: *The Comedy of Errors, 55 Days, The Long Road* and the 2016 co-production of *Observe the Sons of Ulster Marching Towards the Somme* with Headlong and the Abbey, directed by Jeremy Herrin. Chris performed in *Operation Crucible* at the 2018 Brits Off Broadway Festival and its subsequent transfer to the Davenport Theatre, where it was named a *New York Times* Critics' Pick. His screen credits include *The Woman in White* (BBC), *Krypton* (SyFy/E4), *Torvill and Dean* (ITV) and the feature film *Trautmann*, released in 2019.

SOPHIE ROBINSON
LAURA

Sophie was born in Belfast and has trained at LAMDA. *All Mod Cons* will be Sophie's first appearance at the new Lyric Theatre.

Other theatre credits include: *The Yalta Game, The Father, Who's Afraid of Virginia Woolf?* (Gate Theatre, Dublin); *Twelfth Night* (Abbey Theatre); *Juno and the Paycock* (Abbey Theatre/National Theatre London); *The Seagull, The Heretic* (The Lowry, Manchester); *The Lady in the Van* (HullTruck UK Tour); *Electric Dreams* (Battersea Arts Centre). Film, TV and radio credits: *The Good Christian Women's Writing Group, Rebellion* (RTE); *Pick Your Own* (SeeHerePictures Ltd); *The Seedlings*; *Fifteen* (th2ing Production Company); *Mayday* (BBC Radio).

MICHAEL SHEA
GARY

Michael is a relatively recent graduate of LAMDA and comes from Northern Ireland.

Theatre credits include: *Peter and the Starcatcher* (Royal & Derngate), *Desire Under the Elms* (Sheffield Crucible), *Half a Glass of Water* (Theatre 503). Film and television credits include: *Derry Girls, Doctors, Two Angry Men, The Last Letter, Marcella*. Radio Credits include: *Trials of Saint Patrick*.

CREATIVE TEAM

ERICA MURRAY - WRITER

Erica is originally from County Limerick, Ireland. She holds an MFA in Playwriting from the Lir Academy, Trinity College Dublin. She was a member of the Soho Young Writer's Group and the New Playwrights Programme at the Lyric Theatre, Belfast, where she developed *All Mod Cons*. This year she is one of the recipients of the Channel Four Playwrights Scheme bursary award supported by The Peggy Ramsay Foundation. Her first play, *The Cat's Mother*, was long-listed for the Verity Bargate Award, it premiered in 2018 and toured to Underbelly at the Edinburgh Fringe and the Dublin Fringe Festival, where it won the Fishamble Award for Best New Writing.

RONAN PHELAN - DIRECTOR

Ronan Phelan is Associate Director at Rough Magic Theatre Company.

Previous directing credits include: *The Drowned World* (Lir Academy, Dublin); *A Portrait of the Artist as a Young Man* (Rough Magic/ Dublin Theatre Festival); *Merrily We Roll Along* (Lir Academy, Dublin); *Twelfth Night* (LAMDA); *Mr. Burns: A Post-Electric Play* (Rough Magic SEEDS); *Annie* (Cork Opera House); *Much Ado About Nothing* (Lir Academy, Dublin); *The Effect* (Rough Magic); *Inhabitance* (Glassdoll Productions); *To SPACE* (Niamh Shaw); *Assassins* (Rough Magic SEEDS); *LAMBO and Clear_the_Air* (Underscore_Productions); *BROADENING* (Glassdoll Productions); *Pocket Music* (Dublin Fringe 2011, Winner Little Gem Award) and *Durang Durang* (Brazen Tales Theatre Company). He has also directed a radio production of *LAMBO* (RTE Drama On One) which won the PPI Radio Awards Best Drama 2014.

Ronan is a former participant of the Rough Magic SEEDS programme and is a graduate of the DIT Conservatory of Music and Drama. He completed a year as Resident Assistant Director at the Abbey Theatre.

DIANA ENNIS - SET AND COSTUME DESIGN

Diana worked for many years as a Costume Designer before going back to gain her masters in Set Design at the Bristol Old Vic in 2010. She has a long-standing relationship with the Lyric, designing her first show *The Hypochondriac* on the Lyric stage back in 2007. She returned to Northern Ireland in 2011 and has worked extensively in the North, returning to the Lyric many times.

Recent theatre credits include: Costume Design for *Lady Magma* (Premiered in Atelier du Paris touring, choreographer/ director Oona Doherty), Set and Costume for *Bouncers* (The MAC, dir. Zoe Seaton), Set and Costume for *The Elves and the Shoemaker* (The MAC, dir. Paul Mc Eneaney).

Her film credits include: Costume Designer on *Shooting for Socrates* (New Black Films, dir. James Erskin), *Stumpy's Brae* (Six Mile Hill, dir. Chris Baugh) and *The Music Room* (Big Fish Productions, dir. Mick Gordon).

Upcoming projects include: Set and Costume for *Miami Show Band* (Grand Opera House touring, dir. Ruth Carney); Set and Costume for *Space* (The MAC/ Birmingham Rep and tour, dir. Paul McEneaney).

KATIE RICHARDSON - COMPSER & SOUND DESIGN

Katie is heavily involved in the arts as a musician, composer, musical director and facilitator currently based in Belfast. She recently starred in the Lyric's production of *Good Vibrations* as well as being the onstage musical director.

Other previous theatre credits include (as Composer/Musical Director): *Beauty and the Beast* (Lyric Theatre); *The Man Who Fell to Pieces*,*Ubu the King, Huzzies* (Tinderbox); *Hatch* (The Mac); *Flesh Dense, Kissing Marigolds, Dinner, The Weein* (Red Lemon). (As an actor): *Guidelines for a Long and Happy Life* (Tinderbox); *Jack's Last Puff, Dinner, Kissing Marigolds, Tart* (Red Lemon). Katie makes her own music under the name "Hex Hue" (previously Katie and the Carnival/Goldie Fawn) and was a member of Choice-nominated 'Pleasure Beach.' She has supported artists such as BellX1, Noel Gallagher's High Flying Birds, Van Morrison, All Saints, Jesca Hoop, Foy Vance, Duke Special and many more. Katie currently directs several choirs and is in development for a number of new theatre and film projects to be produced and performed in 2019 and beyond.

SARAH JANE SHIELS – LIGHTING DESIGN

SJ began designing lighting in Dublin Youth Theatre, completing a BA in Drama and Theatre Studies 2006 (Trinity), and the Rough Magic SEEDS 3 programme 2006–2008. From 2010–2017, she was co-artistic director of WillFredd Theatre.

Lighting designs include: *Sure Look It, Fuck It* (This Is Pop Baby); *Close Quarters* (Out of Joint/Sheffield Crucible); *FRNKNSTN, Mr Foley the Radio Operator* (Theatre Lovett); *Dolores, Soldier Still, Dusk Ahead* (Junk Ensemble); *East Belfast Boy/Everyday I Wake Up Hopeful* (Prime Cut); *Radio Rosario* (Little John Nee); *Jimmy's Hall, The Remains of Maise Duggan, Town Is Dead* (Abbey Theatre); *Dublin Oldschool* (Project Arts Centre), *Woman Undone, This Beach, Have I No Mouth, The Blue Boy, Silver Stars* (Brokentalkers); *Portrait of the Artist as a Young Man, Midsummer Night's Dream, The Effect, Everything Between Us, The Critic, The House Keeper, Plaza Suite* (Rough Magic); *PALS* (Winner Irish Times Theatre Award Best Lighting 2015); *The Boys of Foley Street, Laundry, World's End Lane, Basin* (ANU Productions). Set and Lighting Designs include: *BEES!, Jockey, CARE, Farm, Follow* (WillFredd Theatre); *How to Keep an Alien* (Sonya Kelly/Rough Magic); *It Folds* (Junk Ensemble/Brokentalkers, Winner Irish Times Theatre Award Best Lighting 2015).

LYRIC
THEATRE

We are delighted to work with Erica Murray to bring the world premiere of her play *All Mod Cons* to the stage.

Erica is the Lyric's Artist-in-Residence for 2019 with the support of the Channel 4 Playwrights' Scheme sponsored by Channel 4 Television and by The Peggy Ramsay Foundation. She is also a previous participant of the Lyric's New Playwrights Programme and a recipient of Fishamble's New Writing Award at the Dublin Fringe.

As a theatre committed to new writing, it's our job at the Lyric to seek out the most exciting new voices in contemporary theatre and provide them with a platform to have their work produced on a national stage.

All Mod Cons has been developed with the support of the Lyric's New Writing department, led by our Literary Manager, Rebecca Mairs. Through the New Playwrights Programme, it provides the next generation of writing talent with the opportunity to develop their work professionally; creating an inviting, dynamic, and inspiring space for new artists to thrive and offering them the support they need to create bold and exciting new work.

Over the past sixty-five years, the Lyric has established itself as Northern Ireland's leading producing theatre, honouring the rich theatrical canon and also premiering the works of playwrights such as Stewart Parker, Martin Lynch, Marie Jones and Christina Reid. We have showcased the talents of Northern Ireland's finest actors, including Adrian Dunbar, Conleth Hill, Stella McCusker, Ciarán Hinds, Frances Tomelty and the Theatre's Patron Liam Neeson, and more recently Aaron McCusker, Rachel Tucker, Seamus O'Hara and Niamh Perry.

The Lyric Theatre is a playhouse for all. We are a shared civic space for artists and audiences alike; a creative hub for theatre-making, nurturing talent and promoting the critical role of the arts in society. Our mission is to create, entertain, and inspire, and it is our great honour to work with Erica to bring her fantastic new play to the stage at the Lyric.

CREATIVE LEARNING MANAGER	PAULINE McKAY
CREATIVE LEARNING SCHOOLS CO-ORDINATOR	ERIN HOEY
HEAD OF CUSTOMER SERVICE	JULIE McKEGNEY
CUSTOMER SERVICE MANAGERS	MARINA HAMPTON
	ASHLENE McGURK
DUTY SUPERVISORS	DÓNAL MORGAN
	HANNAH CONLON
BOX OFFICE SUPERVISOR	EMILY WHITE
BOX OFFICE DEPUTY SUPERVISOR	PAUL McCAFFREY
HOUSEKEEPING	DEBBIE DUFF
	AMANDA RICHARDS
	SAMANTHA WALKER

CUSTOMER SERVICE STAFF
LUCY ARMSTRONG, PAMELA ARMSTRONG, ABBY ATKINSON,
MICHAEL BINGHAM, EMMA BRENNAN, CARLA BRYSON,
SARAH CAREY, PAULA CARSON-LEWIS, HANNAH CONLON,
ELLISON CRAIG, ALACOQUE DAVEY, THOMAS FINNEGAN,
SIMON HALL , HOLLY HANNAWAY, CATHAL HENRY, TERESA HILL ,
HELENNA HOWIE, BECKY HUGHES, MEGAN KEENAN,
GERARD KELLY, FERGAL LINDSAY, MEGAN MAGILL, LAURA
McALEENAN, AOIFE McCLOSKEY, PATRICIA McGREEVY,
MARY McMANUS, CATHAN McROBERTS, CATHERINE MOORE,
DONAL MORGAN, SAMANTHA OBMAN, BERNADETTE OWENS,
BOBBI RAI PURDY, MELISSA RUTNAGUR

VOLUNTEERS
JEAN DUMAS
YVONNE DUMAS
JOAN GORMLEY
RORY McCADDEN
BRONAGH McCALLISTER
EVELINE WILKINSON

LYRIC THEATRE SPONSORS

PRINCIPAL FUNDER

ALSO FUNDED BY

 Belfast
City Council

THE LYRIC THEATRE IS ALSO GENEROUSLY SUPPORTED BY

IN KIND SPONSORS

WITH THANKS TO

To all the staff at the Lyric for making me feel so welcome from the moment I started the residency and before that too. Thanks to Bronagh, Kerry and Clare for being so lovely and letting me distract you in the office and to all the fabulous Marketing Team, Creative Learning Team, Production Team and Front of House Team thanks for working on this play and for making me feel at home. Thank you to Jimmy Fay for being a champion of new work and supporting us every step of the way.

Thank you to Richard Eyre and all the panel of the Channel Four Playwright Scheme and The Peggy Ramsay Foundation for believing in my work and allowing me the best year ever. Thank you to my agent, Jessi and Independent Talent for always being very supportive. A big thank you to Emma, Steven, Felicity and Charlie and all my friends at Samuel French.

To Des Kennedy, Rebecca Root, Kerr Logan, Adele Gribbon and Seamus O'Hara for working on the first reading of this play; your insight was completely invaluable. Thank you so much.

Thanks to Barley for always being so supportive and patient while I was madly redrafting. To Bean for always being at the other end of the line. Thanks to Anna and Jo for always putting me up and being so kind.

To our wonderful cast and creative team-Michael, Mariah, Sophie, and Chris; Katie, Diana and Sarah- it's been a total pleasure to work with every one of you. Thank you for making the world of *All Mod Cons* come alive with such bold talent and skill.

Ronan Phelan; working with you has been a dream come true. I couldn't recommend a better director to be working with a new writer. This play would be nothing without your talent and encouragement. I can't thank you enough.

And Rebecca Mairs. Without your brilliant guidance and enthusiasm this would not be happening. Thank you from the bottom of my heart for seeing the potential in this play during the New Playwright's Programme and for always being hugely supportive and interested in my work. I can't tell you how much it has meant to me.

For my family –
Tommy, Anne, Jack and Luke.

CHARACTERS

GARY – mid-20s, male.

JEAN – 30s, Gary's older sister, trans woman.

IAN – mid-20s, male, their real estate agent and Gary's old friend.

LAURA – late 20s/early 30s, female, one of Ian's other clients.

1.

2C Mount Pleasant Plaza

A very small kitchen-cum-living space in a shoddy two-bedroom flat. Late afternoon.

We open on a long silence as **LAURA** *is surveying the space around her carefully. She's unimpressed.*

IAN *is eagerly watching her, trying not to impose or seem too eager. He tries to glance at his watch.*

Eventually...

LAURA Yeah...

IAN *looks hopeful for a moment. Then the silence returns as* **LAURA** *goes back to examining the room. She is struggling to find the right words.*

It just feels very /cramped?

IAN Cosy?

A beat.

IAN Other people have suggested it's "cosy".

LAURA Have they now?

IAN They have.

She looks around hopelessly.

Take all the time you need.

After a moment of surveying, her eyes land on him again.

LAURA You really remind me of someone.

IAN Do I?

LAURA Yeah, where would I know you from?

IAN Don't think you would.

LAURA It's annoying me now.

IAN Some people say I'm very like that actor, with the hair, you know /him.

LAURA No, it's not him… It'll come to me.

She looks around again. IAN *checks his watch again while she's not looking.* LAURA *lets out a tired sigh.*

Do you have anything smaller?

IAN *(hopeful)* Yes! We do, in fact, lots!

LAURA I was being sarcastic, Ian.

IAN Ah…good one.

LAURA Look, I don't want to take my business elsewhere…

IAN What? No! No, me neither.

LAURA But this really isn't what I'm looking for, is it?

IAN It has a certain charm, and you said you wanted somewhere with character—

LAURA I think we both know asbestos isn't what I meant by "character", is it?

IAN It doesn't have…

LAURA *starts shaking her head and* IAN *mirrors her.*

No.

LAURA No. And I told you on the phone how I really wanted a bath. Is that fair? Do you think that's fair?

LAURA *starts nodding her head and* IAN *mirrors her.*

IAN Yes, of course, I do, but—

LAURA Because none of the flats you've shown me today had one, had they?

IAN No. But—

LAURA And I really don't think that's too much to ask for, is it?

IAN Trust me, Laura, I'm showing you exactly what's on offer in your price range.

LAURA What's the asking on this?

IAN One-sixty. Cash.

LAURA *nearly chokes.*

LAURA Cash? That's insane. I mean that's, that's, that must be a joke?

IAN It's, no, it's not a joke.

LAURA That's literally impossible.

IAN For a location this ideal—

LAURA WE'RE RIGHT ABOVE A FIRE STATION! Sorry. Sorry, for shouting.

IAN That's okay. Safe space.

LAURA But, come on, you can hardly call that "ideal".

IAN It would be if anything were to happen? Like, a hair straightener being left on, or an oven, combusting into flames! You'd be glad of the *ideal* location then.

LAURA I thought there was no oven?

IAN Yes, you'd have to buy one.

LAURA So, it could combust?

IAN Eh—

LAURA Is there an electrical fault, or something?

IAN No, no, no, nothing like that. Not that we know of, anyway!

LAURA Right...

IAN I just meant, you would be very safe if, and that's a big if, *if* anything were to happen.

LAURA I know you're trying to be nice here, but it sounds quite threatening.

IAN I, I don't mean to be, I'm—

LAURA Christ. One-sixty. Cash. How have you sold anything lately?

IAN People always need places to live, I suppose.

LAURA At least I'm not the only fool looking to buy these days.

IAN Not at all, there are lots of you.

> LAURA *glares at him.*

Lots of people looking to buy, I mean.

LAURA And you feel comfortable exploiting them?

IAN I wouldn't say I'm *exploiting* anyone.

LAURA Really? One-sixty. Cash.

IAN I just do as I'm told!

LAURA I don't know how you people live with yourselves. I really don't. I'd be long gone from the property game now, if I was you.

IAN Well, it's a family business, so...can't let the side down!

> *He gives a lack lustre punch into the air.*

LAURA Christ. I think I'd murder my father if I worked for him.

IAN It's my mother's business, actually.

LAURA Oh, of course, sorry. Yeah. Don't know why I...

> LAURA *is annoyed at herself for assuming that.* IAN *checks his watch.*

Do you have somewhere to be?

IAN No! No...em. Maybe have one more look around and we'll call it a day?

She slowly looks around. Her mind wanders elsewhere...

LAURA The flat with the lino in the kitchen...

IAN Yes. The first one this morning?

LAURA Could we have a look at that one again?

A beat.

IAN Now?

LAURA Yeah?

IAN You mean the one on the other side of town?

LAURA Yes... Is that a problem?

IAN *(it clearly is not okay)* No. No problem at all!

2.

98 Linton Avenue

JEAN is sitting across from GARY in the living room of their mother's house.

JEAN It was really, really beautiful.

GARY Thank you.

JEAN You did an amazing job.

GARY I don't know about that...

JEAN You did, you spoke so eloquently.

GARY That's good.

JEAN Who helped you with the speech?

A beat.

GARY No one?

JEAN Really?

GARY You sound surprised.

JEAN No, no, I'm just... It was brilliant, it just...it didn't sound like you.

GARY What does that mean?

JEAN In a good way, I mean!

GARY How is that good if my mother's eulogy doesn't sound like it was written by me?

JEAN *Our* mother.

GARY Sure...whatever...

JEAN I just didn't realise you had so many...

GARY Feelings?

JEAN I was going to say "words".

Pause.

GARY I might have used the synonym function a few times.

JEAN "Her *dogmatic* views on the world".

GARY There's only so many times you can use the word "stubborn". You try writing a eulogy, fucksake, see how you get on.

JEAN I was just trying to make you laugh. She would have been so proud of you, Gary, okay? For doing that today. I was so proud of you.

GARY I don't need you to be proud of me.

JEAN Okay, sure.

GARY But...yeah, thanks.

JEAN It was a really beautiful speech, honestly.

GARY So, you think people liked it?

JEAN I think people loved it.

GARY I mean, I tried my best... There's only so much you can... Like, words can only get you so far, you know? There's a lot more I...

He covers his face in his hands.

Sorry.

JEAN Oh, Gary...come here.

JEAN *gets up and tries to comfort him.* GARY *recoils.*

GARY No, no, please don't...

A moment between them, a hesitation.

I just need some space. I'm, I'm fine.

JEAN Sure.

GARY Thanks though.

A silence.

JEAN It's freezing in here.

GARY I suppose we could turn the heating on? Now that she won't know...

JEAN Would you mind?

GARY No. No, not at all. I've been dying to do it for years!

They sort of smile, shared experiences.

JEAN I guess that's one plus side.

GARY *stops smiling.*

Sorry. That was insensitive. I'll go turn it on.

GARY *is on his own. He looks at the chair his mother used to sit in.* JEAN *returns.*

That felt sort of symbolic.

GARY I was going around inside wearing a scarf and gloves last winter.

JEAN I can imagine.

JEAN *casually sits down in their mother's chair. This freaks* GARY *out.*

GARY Em. Can you not? Can you not sit there?

JEAN Here?

GARY Yeah, eh, it's just...it's freaking me out a bit.

JEAN Why?

GARY That's her chair!

JEAN Right, of course. Sorry!

GARY No, no, absolutely fine, I'm sorry. Eh, sorry to be weird.

JEAN *has moved seat. A silence again.*

JEAN You know...the priest said "John" after the eulogy. Survived by her two kids; Gary and John. And I was wondering if–

GARY I didn't know he was going to say that. I told him, Jean.

JEAN I just wanted to check.

GARY No, I know, I was going to say that to you...em. Later. But I did think it at the time.

JEAN It's alright. I mean...

GARY I'll have a word with him.

JEAN There's no point, honestly, it was embarrassing, but look. Won't happen again.

GARY I'll call him tomorrow. Make him apologise.

JEAN You don't need to threaten a priest, Gary!

GARY I never said threaten, did I?

JEAN It's fine, honestly. I sort of braced myself for it coming back here.

GARY You know, people are more accepting here than you think.

JEAN Really?

GARY It's a very different country now than it was when you left.

JEAN I hope so.

GARY Honestly, people here are cool with...whatever. Anything!

JEAN Well, I'll be the judge of that.

GARY And if you do get any hassle, like, you let me know. I'll sort them out.

JEAN I'll be fine, Gar. Thank you.

GARY Honestly. I mean that.

JEAN Hopefully that won't be necessary. Although in this area...
Christ, who knows.

GARY You should feel safe in your own home.

JEAN Not everyone has that privilege, I guess.

GARY Well, they should.

A pause.

Look, I have to show you something.

GARY *pulls out a tin of biscuits from under their mother's
chair.* JEAN *looks confused.*

Me and Mam had been saving up some money over the
years. Bit by bit, like.

JEAN And you splashed out on a tin of biscuits?

GARY Listen to me, Jean. I'm being serious.

JEAN Sorry.

GARY There's in or around twenty-five grand inside of this
tin. In cash.

JEAN What?

GARY Twenty-five grand. In or around...

JEAN Wait, no. You both saved money in a tin of biscuits?

GARY Do you want to judge, or do you want to listen?

JEAN Sorry, sorry. Em...okay, this is a lot of money.

GARY I know.

JEAN How the hell did you manage to save that much? *In cash?*

GARY I might have done a few odd jobs cash in hand, and I used
to give her some rent money, but she obviously tucked it
away in here. Plus, her not turning on the heating, that
kind of thing.

JEAN Can I have a look?

GARY *nods solemnly.* JEAN *approaches and* GARY *lets her peak inside.*

Wow. That's, that's in or around twenty-five grand alright.

GARY That's what I said.

JEAN So, what are you showing it to me for?

GARY She wanted me to use it to buy a new place.

JEAN For the two of you?

GARY For myself. She always said she wanted me to own my own home, eventually. You know, like she owned this one. It was important to her.

JEAN Okay.

GARY So, I was thinking...now that you're back. For good, like. We could maybe buy somewhere. Together. If you were up for it? I could pay the deposit and we could use your salary to pay the mortgage.

A pause. JEAN *considers.*

JEAN Really?

GARY Only if you wanted to, like.

JEAN I... It's just a big thing to ask.

GARY Yeah, like I said, only if you wanted to, I don't care either way.

JEAN You'd really want to move from here?

GARY That was always the plan and now... Look, I don't think I can keep living here with her gone. The last few days I just... I think I need, you know...

JEAN A fresh start.

GARY Yeah, that. And I know you don't like being back here either—

JEAN It's not that I don't like it, it's more...

GARY Jean.

JEAN Yeah, no, I really don't like it. It's weird.

GARY Well, then.

He waits.

What do you think?

JEAN I think... I think that makes sense.

GARY It does.

JEAN But is it not too soon?

GARY I want to be out of here as soon as I can.

JEAN Are you sure? It seems sudden.

GARY I'm very sure. If you'd be ready, that is?

JEAN I was ready eight years ago.

GARY So...

JEAN So...yes. Yeah. Let's do it!

GARY Great. Great! It's happening.

JEAN It's happening. Exciting!

A pause. Neither of them really knows what to say next...

GARY So, what do you think we should do first?

JEAN Honestly, the first thing would be to put that money in the bank. I feel uncomfortable even being around it in a bloody biscuit tin. By the way, how did you both have the restraint to not eat through the first layer?

GARY Too stale.

JEAN Right.

GARY She bought it second-hand.

JEAN Second-hand biscuits?

GARY Don't ask... Actually, do you want a cup of tea? All this talk of...

JEAN Sure. I can make it.

GARY No, no, I'll do it.

GARY gets up to go to the kitchen.

We only have almond milk, is that okay?

JEAN That's perfect.

GARY I can go to the shop and get some normal if you?

JEAN No, no, honestly. Almond is /fine.

GARY Cool.

JEAN I'm just surprised! This is coming from "the chicken nugget monster".

GARY I haven't eaten a nugget in a long time. I'm actually a vegetarian most days. And I'm avoiding lactose.

JEAN Why? Is it awkward between you two?

GARY rolls his eyes.

Of course. Sorry, it's just funny, because when I left you were on about two McFlurries a day and now—

GARY That was a long time ago.

JEAN I know it was, I'm not saying that—

GARY People change. Especially when you don't see them for a long time.

JEAN Of course, of course they do, eh, sorry.

GARY turns to go. Then –.

GARY Jean?

JEAN Yeah?

GARY Look, thanks. For coming back, like.

JEAN We're going to make this work, Gary, okay?

GARY Yeah, no, I, eh... *(clears throat)* I am glad you're here. After all.

3.

2C Mount Pleasant Plaza

The same kitchen-cum-living area we first met IAN *in.*
Evening time.

GARY *is shamelessly studying the room in front of* IAN.

GARY So this is one of your flats?

IAN I've been showing it all week, it's a fucking nightmare.,
isn't it?

GARY No, no, it's eh...it's cosy.

IAN Thank you! Yes, that's what I've been telling them. You
sure you don't want a beer?

GARY Positive. Trying to stay off alcohol, keep the old head clear.

IAN Good for you.

GARY Thanks for, eh, meeting me here.

IAN Not at all, it's good to see you out and about. How have
you been?

GARY Ah, you know...

IAN *thinks he might elaborate but* GARY *lets this vague*
comment hang for a few moments.

IAN I was so sorry to hear about your poor Mam, Gary.

GARY Yeah, yeah... One of those things...

IAN I had no idea she was sick even?

GARY No. No one did.

IAN And are you feeling...?

GARY Keeping the head above water. What more could you ask?

IAN Right, yeah.

GARY I mean, what can you do? Circle of life, and all that...

IAN Yeah, totally. What goes around comes around.

GARY That's a different thing.

IAN Oh, yeah.

GARY You're just naming a song?

IAN Yeah, no, ignore me. Sorry.

GARY S'grand.

> IAN *gears himself up to say this –.*

IAN But look, man, if you ever want to talk to someone, I'm always here if you need me.

> *A silence.* GARY *ignores him and is intent on staring at something imaginary on the floor.*

GARY Sure look, go on then, I might have one of those beers.

IAN That's the stuff.

> IAN *goes to retrieve two beers.* GARY *composes himself.* IAN *brings them over and hands him one.*

GARY Good to see you, man.

IAN You too, man. Get that into you now.

GARY Men!

IAN Men!

> *They cheers and drink. This strange exchange is probably something their friends have done since their underage drinking days.*

> GARY *is about to drink again but stops when* IAN *says –.*

I like your man bun.

GARY It's just a "bun", Ian. You don't need to say the "man" part, that's old-fashioned.

IAN Right, gotcha.

GARY Just a hairstyle, like. No big deal.

IAN I was thinking of getting an earring, myself.

GARY What? Ian. Don't do that.

IAN Why not?

GARY You'd look like a fuckin' gangster wearing that suit with an earring. You couldn't pull it off. You'd never sell a house again looking like that.

IAN Ah, you're probably right.

He drinks. Resigned to his life with no piercings.

So, you back working?

GARY Sort of. I'm on a kind of freelance-part-timey-contract-yoke. So, bits of stuff, yeah.

IAN Cool, cool. Well, now that I have a professional around what do you think of the electrics in here?

GARY *half-heartedly looks up and around at the light fixtures, as if he's asked this all the time.*

GARY Look good to me.

IAN Good!

GARY I'll have to charge you for that now.

IAN Ha, yes. Send me the invoice! Ha, good one.

GARY *smiles but doesn't keep the joke alive.*

I'd say you get loads of women calling you up, do you?

GARY What do you mean?

IAN Asking you how to fix their tellies or screw in a lightbulb, that kind of thing.

GARY *does not get what* IAN *is trying to imply.*

GARY Not really. I'm contracted by a company, so they just call me into their office when something needs to be sorted.

IAN Right, yeah.

GARY I'd say it's probably sixty-forty, men to women.

IAN Nice.

GARY Who work there, like.

IAN Course.

GARY And I don't fix televisions.

IAN Gotcha.

IAN *has a guzzle of beer to fill another silence.*

I haven't seen the lads in ages.

GARY No? A lot of them were at the funeral.

IAN You got my messages about that, right? I was trying to get there on time, I really was, but I was stuck with this client all day and by the time I got rid of her I knew it would be over.

GARY Honestly, don't worry about it, it was a small thing anyway, intimate.

IAN Beautiful. Did you have to say anything?

GARY I did yeah... Did the whole eulogy, and eh, it sort of brought the house down.

IAN You're great at that stuff. Remember when you did that poem standing up in front of the whole school? The one about the frog?

GARY It was nothing like that, Ian. This was a serious thing.

IAN Yeah, no, course not.

GARY Even caught Jean wiping away a few tears.

IAN Jean? Jean. Yes. Yes! How is that?

GARY It's fine?

IAN So they're back?

GARY Now you're making it sound like there's two of her.

IAN Sorry! I don't know the correct way to...

GARY Think of it this way: she is a she. No confusion. Easy to remember.

IAN Right, yeah, no, of course. It's cool. I actually have an uncle in San Francisco who has a friend who is...

He thinks the better of going down this road.

I understand, honestly!

GARY Good.

IAN So have the lads met her?

GARY She's the same person, Ian!

IAN Right, sorry, I know.

GARY S'grand.

IAN And had your Mam seen Jean before she...

GARY Yeah, yeah, Mam went over for a weekend to Berlin sometime last year.

IAN That's nice.

GARY Yeah, I think that gives Jean a lot of comfort.

IAN Course. So, she's back living here? For good, like?

GARY Yeah, well, that's what I wanted to talk to you about. Because we're looking to buy somewhere. A place to live, like.

IAN Right. At the moment?

GARY Yes and we need someone to advise us. We need help. We'd like you to be our...

IAN Real estate agent?

GARY Person. Yeah. If you're too busy or whatever, it's grand.

IAN Not at all! I'd be happy to assist in any way I can. And you know, things are bad out there, but they aren't...bad, bad! People talk it up.

GARY What do you mean?

IAN I mean, you know, people are hesitant, at the moment, to buy.

GARY Why's that?

IAN Have you been keeping up with the news lately?

GARY I've been kind of busy, Ian?

IAN Of course! Never mind all that. We'll find you somewhere. Leave all that to me.

GARY I'm thinking we want to move fairly soon too.

IAN Alright, very cool, what's your timeline?

GARY Say, a month? Two months?

IAN You've never done this before, have you?

GARY Why?

IAN That's basically impossible. Six months would be doing really well.

GARY Six months it is so.

IAN Alright, challenge accepted! To six months!

Cheers.

GARY Men!

IAN Men!

They drink. The beers are dwindling.

So, what's happening to your mother's house?

GARY We're going to keep it until we find somewhere new. Then sell it on.

IAN Well, if you need someone.

IAN *points to himself.*

GARY One thing at a time, I think. Let's take it easy.

IAN So, was this Jean's idea or what?

GARY No. Why?

IAN I just can't imagine you living anywhere but that house.

GARY Well, it was my idea. Moving out.

IAN Good for you!

GARY Yeah, I just don't like being there when Mam's gone.

This is accidentally too deep for the two of them to handle. IAN *breaks it.*

IAN What about this place? It's a two-bed?

GARY I thought you just said it was a fucking nightmare?

IAN Did I say that?

GARY I don't want to live over a fire station, Ian. Do you understand me, here?

IAN I do. I'll look after you two, Gary. Trust me. And can I just say: thank you for giving me this opportunity.

GARY Jesus, you're not pissed after one beer, are you?

IAN Sorry, I didn't mean to sound so corny. Ah! Just thanks. Thanks for giving me a shot.

GARY *downs the rest of his beer.*

GARY Ah listen, Iano, it's all good. Right, I'm going to head off but see you...

IAN Whenever you guys are ready, give me a shout. I'll start compiling a list.

GARY Of what?

IAN Houses?

GARY Yes. Good. Sound.

GARY *goes to head off.* IAN *hesitantly calls after him.*

IAN And you have had your mortgage approved, right?

GARY Jean's in charge of all the...technical stuff.

IAN Great, I'll ask her.

GARY And look, when you do meet her. Just don't act like a fucking...dick. Alright?

IAN How would I... No, I won't.

4.

98 Linton Avenue

Boxes lie around the living room of GARY *and* JEAN'*s mother's house.* JEAN *is sorting out old stuff.* GARY *enters eating Coco Pops, wearing his boxers and a T-shirt.*

GARY Morning. What's going on here?

JEAN Afternoon!

GARY Don't be at me. What's all this?

JEAN I'm moving some stuff into boxes.

GARY What stuff?

JEAN From her room. I can't sleep in there knowing all this crap is under the bed.

GARY That's not crap. That's our stuff.

JEAN I found two old Radiohead albums. Do you still listen to them?

GARY Sometimes.

JEAN We don't even have a CD player in the house?

GARY Lots of this stuff has sentimental value, okay?

JEAN Like the weight's bench that's now in my old room? I can't even open the door properly to get in. Do you ever use it?

GARY Yes!

JEAN It looked pretty dusty to me...

GARY You can sleep in my room instead if you really can't sleep there?

JEAN When's the last time you hoovered your room?

Pause. GARY *thinks back. He's never hoovered his room.*

GARY I can do it today.

JEAN It'll be useful when we move anyway, to have this done.

GARY Just don't throw anything out. Until I say you can.

JEAN Alright... I'll make a pile. Have you seen Margaret?

GARY Margaret! Speaking of random pieces of crap?

JEAN She's not crap!

GARY She's a mermaid Barbie with a buzzcut and a demonic smile.

JEAN I've been searching for her everywhere, up in the attic and everything, no sign of her anywhere.

GARY I haven't seen her in years... She's not in one of those boxes?

JEAN No. I checked.

GARY Mam must have thrown her out.

JEAN She wouldn't have done that.

GARY Wouldn't she?

JEAN You don't know where she is?

GARY No, I told you.

JEAN I thought she would have kept her in the box with Special Blankie?

GARY Special Blankie?

JEAN Yeah. Do you want to see him?

GARY *(yes, he does)* No!

JEAN *(reading his mind)* Well, it's just here if you want to have a look at it.

She rests it on top of one of the boxes. GARY *tries not to look at it.*

GARY Whatever.

JEAN I think Margaret will show up, I doubt Mam would have thrown her out.

GARY I guess you can't expect someone to keep your things if you abandon them for eight years and a bit.

JEAN Alright, how long have you been keeping that in the chamber?

GARY Just saying.

JEAN I didn't abandon you. I told you both when I was leaving.

GARY No, I'm just saying that's what it felt like from our perspective.

JEAN "Our perspective"? Gary, we kept in touch!

GARY Right, yeah, the awkward phone calls every six months. Loved those.

JEAN You could have come to visit me?

GARY You could have come home at Christmas time?

JEAN Maybe I didn't feel like you wanted me to come home?

GARY Maybe that's because you're the one who decided to leave?

JEAN I left because I had to. I don't expect you to understand that.

GARY I understand! Don't talk to me like I'm a child.

JEAN Then don't eat your kids' cereal in your fucking underpants then!

A pause. They both realise this has ventured into slightly humorous territory.

Sorry.

GARY No, no, I mean...it is a kids' cereal.

JEAN Honestly, the amount of sugar in that...

GARY Jean. Please.

JEAN Sorry. Yes. You do you.

She goes back to sorting out the boxes of old stuff.

Oh wow. Another treasure.

JEAN *holds up a cushion with a slogan cross-stitched onto its cover.*

GARY She made that herself last year. She was planning on giving it to you if you came home for Christmas.

JEAN Well, now I feel awful.

GARY It's a cushion. A pillow, like, to use to sleep on or put on your couch or something.

JEAN I know what a cushion is, Gary. "Home is where you hang your heart" ...Jesus. Was it supposed to be a dig?

GARY Probably.

JEAN Thank God for the lump sum, otherwise I might be using it to smother myself.

GARY That's horrible.

JEAN Come on. If you can't laugh...

GARY *still looks stony-faced.*

Just a joke, Gar.

GARY You shouldn't joke about that stuff.

A beat. They both look at the pillow.

I always hated that phrase: "Home is where you hang your heart". It makes me imagine wrenching out your own heart and hanging it on a nail or something.

GARY *shudders.*

JEAN That's some imagination you've got going there.

GARY Hanging you heart, like? Do you not think?

JEAN Well, now I'm not going to be able to look at it without thinking that.

GARY Count yourself lucky. She got me that Australia snow globe.

JEAN When did she go there?

GARY She didn't. Found it in a charity shop, I presume.

JEAN Does Australia even get snow?

GARY I'm pretty sure it doesn't.

JEAN Wow... I'm sorry. She was never a great one for presents.

GARY No, she wasn't. You know, when she came back from visiting you in Berlin, she brought me back a packet of chocolate euros and I was thinking *(He is really trying not to cry into his cereal now)* you can buy those anywhere, it's not specifically a German thing, like.

A good pause.

JEAN I'm surprised you're only bringing this up now.

GARY What was she like?

JEAN What do you mean?

GARY While she was over there?

JEAN I...

GARY She told me she had the most amazing time.

JEAN She said that?

GARY Yeah. I picked her up from the airport. She said she had a brilliant time.

JEAN Really?

GARY Yeah. And I never asked her much more about it because... I didn't really want to know, at the time. Because I was, well... I suppose I was jealous of you.

JEAN Jealous! Why on earth?

GARY Because you got to spend proper time with her.

JEAN Gary. You saw her every day?

GARY Yeah, but I never went on holidays with her, as an adult like. I always meant to. I always meant to bring her somewhere for her birthday or a long weekend. But, I don't know why, I just never got around to it. But I wish I had spent time with her like that, not just buzzing in and out for dinner and tea. Or doing jobs for her. It would have been great to go away, travelling or something together. Then I would have seen her like you did; just having fun.

JEAN You two were so close, Gar. You know that. And no one goes travelling with their Mam when they're in their twenties, come on.

GARY I just wish I had come with her so the three of us could have been together at least. What kind of stuff did you get up to?

JEAN Ah, you know, the usual Berlin stuff; did a walking tour, saw the wall, then she dropped a pill and got into Berghain.

GARY Seriously?

JEAN No! We...we went for some walks.

GARY With her dodgy knee?

JEAN Small walks. Short walks. And we sat outside cafes and... had drinks! And ate food. And laughed. And stayed up late talking.

GARY That sounds really nice.

JEAN It was.

GARY I'm glad, Jean, that you got to see her before she...

JEAN Me too. Now, enough of this...wallowing, or whatever we're doing! We're meeting Ian today, right?

GARY Half two. And just ignore him if he starts acting like a bit of a dope.

JEAN What do you mean?

GARY You'll see...

JEAN You're still sure you're ready to do this?

GARY Very, very sure.

JEAN Then you won't mind if I throw out Special Blankie?

GARY can pick up his special blanket and look at it during this transition if it feels appropriate.

5.

17 Manilla Walk

An unimpressive house they are viewing. IAN *is showing around his client,* LAURA.

LAURA So, you're telling me people have actually lived here?

IAN I've seen it done before.

LAURA I can barely breath, in this room, Ian, with the two of us in it.

IAN That could be an advantage?

LAURA Tell me how?

IAN Less air to heat up during the colder months of the year. Lower the heating bill?

LAURA It's minus one outside and I feel like I'm in a lizard cage.

IAN Could that be a good thing?

LAURA Living in a lizard cage? What do you think?

IAN I think it's honestly a great first-time buyer offer. Once we fix the heating situation.

LAURA And where are my kids supposed to sleep?

IAN You don't have any kids?

LAURA How do you know?

IAN I just presumed from your...do you?

LAURA No, but I want to, someday. And where would they fit? You can't be telling me this is all you have to offer in my price range? I'm been saving for years, Ian. Years. I opened a savings account for this moment when I was twenty-two. Twenty fucking two.

IAN Well, if you've only been saving for a year then what do you expect?

This lame attempt at a compliment falls completely flat.

LAURA I'm really not in the mood today for your commentary.

IAN Absolutely. Sorry about...

IAN *clears his throat in an attempt to change his personality...*

Have you seen the third bedroom?

LAURA I didn't think there was one?

IAN It's under the stairs.

LAURA I thought that was a cupboard.

IAN Yes, it could be a big cupboard, or have you seen those IKEA bunk beds?

LAURA Oh Jesus. I really don't know how many more of these I can view... I need to sit down. Sorry, I'm feeling kind of... Can you open a window or something?

IAN There aren't any windows.

LAURA What? Surely that's some kind of breach of human rights?

IAN I've checked and...it's not.

LAURA I have a right to sunlight, Ian. I must have?

IAN Unfortunately...no.

LAURA No windows? In a living room?

IAN They're increasingly hard to come by these days. But think of it this way: you might not be affected by daylight savings?

LAURA I think I'd prefer to live with my parents forever than spend another five minutes in this room. And they are hard people to live with, Ian. They are difficult people.

Her expression tells **IAN** *she has seen things...*

IAN Well, that's a big statement. Especially for a woman of...?

LAURA You really want to try to guess my age?

IAN I was going to say, "of your calibre".

LAURA Calibre?

IAN Yes, professional. Important.

LAURA I really need to stop seeing you so much.

IAN That's what my last girlfriend said too.

LAURA Excuse me?

IAN That was a joke! Because you said...

LAURA Can we just cut the crap here for a second. You need to show me somewhere decent soon otherwise I'm going with another agent. Is that clear?

IAN Loud and clear. I think you'll really like the next one I have for you.

LAURA Good.

GARY *(offstage)* Ian? Is this the one? Ian?

IAN Yes, push the door!

Nothing happens.

I'll go get him.

IAN *goes to get* **GARY**. **LAURA** *starts sniffing the air, suspiciously.* **IAN** *and* **GARY** *come in.*

GARY Woah, it's hot in here.

IAN Well, it's very cold outside, so it's all relative. You'll aclimatise in a few minutes. Won't he, Laura?

LAURA You're looking at this place too?

GARY It looks like it.

IAN I told you, it's highly sought-after.

LAURA I don't know what to believe anymore...

GARY I take it you're not going to make a bid?

LAURA No. Not in a million years.

Awkward pause.

Are you looking for a two-bed?

GARY Yes! Two-bed minimum.

LAURA Same as myself.

GARY Cool.

LAURA What's your budget if you don't mind me asking?

IAN You know, it's unprofessional to have two clients here at the same time. I think it's best if you...if we keep it separate.

He tries to usher LAURA *out or stands in front of her blocking* GARY.

LAURA I'll leave you to it, so. Think I've seen enough for one day. Ian, I'll be calling your office tomorrow.

IAN I look forward to it!

LAURA Nice to meet you. Good luck with it all.

GARY Thanks, eh, you too.

LAURA *leaves.*

IAN Sorry about her, she's a bit of a negative person.

GARY No worries.

IAN Is Jean not coming too?

GARY Yeah, she's on her way. Just dropping the biscuit tin off at the bank.

A pause.

IAN Is that a kind of a euphemism or...?

GARY No...?

He doesn't elaborate.

So, this place?

IAN It's new on the market as of last week. Quite something, isn't it?

GARY There's a kind of a smell... Do you get that?

IAN No?

GARY *takes a deep sniff in.*

GARY Are you really not getting that?

IAN I might have adapted to it.

JEAN *(offstage)* Hello? Is this number seventeen? Gary?

GARY Yeah, in here!

IAN Push the door!

JEAN *enters.*

JEAN Ian. MacMahon. I would not have recognised you!

They hug. **IAN** *is about to say the exact same thing, but stops himself.*

IAN Yes, I grew up! And I lost a lot of weight in the process.

JEAN It suits you. How are you?

IAN Good, good!

JEAN You look so different. In a good way!

IAN So do you! Obviously, I mean...you look amazing!

JEAN You're too kind.

IAN No, really, not that you didn't look nice before, because you did. Just...wow.

GARY Sorry, Jean. Ian, just chill out a bit, would you?

JEAN Not at all! I don't mind one bit. Let's call a shovel a shovel, shall we?

GARY I think you mean spade?

IAN Sorry, I didn't mean to offend anyone?

JEAN You're not offending me.

GARY Can we just talk about the house hunt?

JEAN Ian, we can continue this later.

   IAN *goes bright red.*

GARY Jesus.

IAN I don't really have anything else to say.

GARY She was joking. Let's just get down to business.

IAN Right. Right! So, I know you both wanted to start looking immediately and I do have a lot of unusual but exciting properties to show you. But before we start today, I wanted to say, something I say to all my clients which is, basically: *(clears his throat, loving being the centre of attention)* house-hunting can be a tense time. Especially if you're doing it in a rush like you two are and especially if you've had a particularly stressful period recently like...

GARY Our mother dying.

IAN Well, yes. Sorry, I didn't mean to bring it up again, only I give this talk to everyone who starts the search in a rush. Not that it's out of the ordinary or anything, just, I mean... you need to be prepared for the time ahead. It's hard work finding a house that suits you both, is what I mean. So, open the minds, be prepared for the unexpected, and of course, number one thing to remember: compromise is key. That all sound good?

JEAN We'll be fine. I'm sure.

GARY Let's just get on with it.

IAN Okey-dokey. So, after I reviewed your budget, it slightly reduces the amount of properties on offer. But, for the first place on our "hunt"? What do you think?

He makes a big sweeping gesture around the room as if it is a palace.

JEAN Oh? This is a... I thought this was your office?

IAN I wish!

JEAN I was wondering why there was no desk.

IAN Full disclosure, it was an office, but we decided to show it as a flat since it's such a great location. I mean, it would be ridiculous to miss this opportunity.

JEAN Yes, there are a lot of office buildings around here?

IAN And a Lidl!

JEAN But my first instinct is that I think I'd like somewhere a bit less...horrible.

GARY Yeah, I absolutely hate it in here.

IAN Okay. I'll take all that on board. "Less horrible".

GARY I want somewhere with at least one window.

JEAN Yeah, I second that. At least one window would be nice.

IAN Everyone does. They are very hard to come by these days. Now enlighten me more, what would your ideal apartment look like?

GARY It would look like a house. I don't want to die in a crummy flat.

IAN Is there something I should know about?

GARY No! I just don't want to have to move again after we find this new place, I want it to be our home. Like it would be weird moving from a house to an apartment, you know what I mean? I'm not sure I'm ready to down size.

IAN Okay, what about yourself, Jean?

JEAN I don't personally mind a flashy apartment.

GARY I'm looking for a proper house kind of home. Two beds minimum. Max...maybe four. But I'd be happy with five.

IAN Are you aware of the budget you gave me?

GARY Yeah, Jean told me.

JEAN I'll take him through it again.

IAN Have you looked at any houses on the internet? Seen what's out there?

GARY I thought that's what you're doing for us?

JEAN I've had a look, yes.

IAN Okay, well, I'll do my best! We can have a look at a mixture of houses and apartments. All good?

GARY *looks to* JEAN.

JEAN Yep!

GARY Fine.

IAN Let the good times roll, people!

This falls incredibly flat.

Does anyone want to have a look at the bedrooms?

6.

98 Linton Avenue

GARY *and* JEAN *are at home, it's late at night. They are both on the couch playing a game of Guess Who?.*

GARY Is he wearing a hat?

JEAN No.

GARY *flicks down a few heads on the board.*

Does yours have a beard?

GARY No. He doesn't have *a beard.*

JEAN *flicks down three heads on the board.*

Does yours look smart and kind of serious?

JEAN Gary?

GARY What?

JEAN That's way too subjective. It's based on appearances.

GARY Well, does he *appear* smart and serious?

JEAN *regards her chosen character.*

JEAN He's wearing glasses, if that's what you mean?

GARY *flicks down a few, happy he's getting closer.*

Is yours Frank?

GARY Yes! Shit.

JEAN You asked me not to go easy on you...

GARY How did you know?

JEAN You *always* pick him.

GARY No, I don't?

JEAN You used to always pick him.

GARY I like his moustache.

JEAN Also, you're still such a cheater!

GARY How am I cheating?

JEAN Saying "no" when I asked about the beard?

GARY *Moustache* not beard. Be more specific.

JEAN Okay, if you could be one of them, who would you be?

GARY Definitely Derek.

JEAN Derek!

GARY Look at his mohawk, he doesn't give a fuck.

JEAN I'd be Megan, I think.

GARY No, Megan is so unhappy.

JEAN She's smiling?

GARY But not with her eyes.

JEAN How did we spend so many hours playing this as kids?

GARY Well, in fairness, it's a solid two-player. Another round?

JEAN No, I'm going to bed.

GARY Ah, come on! Best out of three?

JEAN Absolutely not. Are you not wrecked after today?

GARY A bit, yeah.

JEAN You should go to bed too, we've another four more tomorrow.

GARY *flicks a few characters on the game, fed up.*

GARY Who knew this would be such a trek?

JEAN *finds this sweet, since everyone knew this was going to be a "trek"…*

JEAN Let's not give up just yet.

GARY It's just so *boring*. I didn't think it would be this boring. Did you?

JEAN Maybe we should drink our way through it tomorrow.

GARY Actually, some of the lads are going for pints in the evening, if you want to join?

JEAN Oh, yeah? Do I know any of them?

GARY Lads from school. Kevin and them. Ian will probably tag along too, as usual.

JEAN I think you should be nicer to poor Ian. He's trying his best.

GARY I'm very nice to Ian! We all are.

JEAN He seems, I don't know, lonely, or something.

GARY Ah, he's grand.

JEAN Does he have a girlfriend?

GARY *finds this funny.*

GARY No! Why?

JEAN Just wondering.

GARY Please tell me you're not interested in Ian. That would be the last thing—

JEAN Jesus, no! He's not my type. Trust me.

GARY Good.

Beat.

Who is your type? If you had to pick from *Guess Who*?

JEAN Steve, definitely.

GARY Steve! But he's ginger?

JEAN Yeah? He has a nice smile.

GARY I'd go for Jane.

JEAN Ugh. That's such an obvious choice.

GARY Why?

JEAN You just picked her because she's the only one wearing a boob tube.

GARY No! I happen to think she has a nice personality...

JEAN *throws something at him.*

JEAN You're a swine.

A pause.

Are you seeing anyone, at the moment?

GARY Besides Jane?

JEAN Besides fictional characters in a children's board game. Yes.

GARY Mmm... Not really.

JEAN Not really?

GARY Well, I'm on the apps.

JEAN Skulking around.

GARY Exactly... What about you?

JEAN No apps. No person either. I was seeing someone back in... but he was a good bit older and I was moving back anyway, so, it just...

GARY You didn't break up just to come back here, did you?

JEAN No, no, it was fizzling anyway.

GARY How long were ye together?

JEAN About a year.

GARY So, it was serious?

JEAN   Nah. It never really got serious, that was the issue.

GARY   Did Mam meet him?

JEAN   Oh, no, no.

GARY   Why not?

JEAN   Eh, do you remember how she used to act when I brought someone around here?

GARY   Mmm. Bit of a liability...

JEAN   Yeah, I didn't think I'd bother with all the introductions.

GARY   I wish I had been there. I know I keep saying that, but I do. Everyone else seems to be able to hang out as a family all the time. Wish we had too.

JEAN   Oh, Gary, it wasn't a big deal, really. You didn't miss much.

GARY   No, seriously. I have this picture in my head now of the two of you sitting outside restaurants and cafes drinking sangria and eating tapas. I like thinking about that.

JEAN   You know, those are both Spanish things, right?

GARY   You know what I mean! I just like thinking about it; my Mam and my sister, having a nice time together. I can imagine you making her laugh so hard you can see all her fillings, like when we were small.

JEAN   I don't remember ever making her laugh.

GARY   You did, all the time.

A moment.

GARY   I might go visit her, in between viewings, tomorrow. I think one of the flats is close to her spot.

JEAN   Good plan.

GARY Do you want to come too?

JEAN If you want me to.

GARY I think I'd like that.

A pause.

JEAN Go on so... Best out of three!

GARY *does a small "yess!" motion with his fist.*

7a.

28 Crescent Court

IAN *is alone. He is on the phone to his mother.*

IAN Yes, Mam, I know. No, I do. I understand. I do, I said.
I will. I am doing it now. Yes, now. No, they are coming
in now so I can't... I meant now as in later. Why is that a
problem? But why can't I?

*JEAN enters behind IAN. She notices he is on the phone
so doesn't disturb him.*

Alright, sorry. I said sorry! I said...

She has hung up.

Aah, fuck it. Fuck her!

JEAN Everything okay?

IAN Ah! Jesus. Sorry didn't hear you come in.

JEAN No, I should have knocked. I just tried the door and it
was open so—

IAN Course, no, come in and make yourself at home! Ignore
the carpet, if you can.

JEAN Yes, it's quite the statement choice.

IAN I really don't understand what goes on in people's minds,
sometimes.

JEAN No, me neither.

Pause.

IAN So is Gary...?

JEAN He said he'd meet me here. Had some mysterious appointment this afternoon.

IAN I see. The international man of mystery!

JEAN Indeed. Although I'd drop the international part.

IAN Ha, unless you'd count his yearly pilgrimage to Ibiza.

JEAN You're right! International indeed.

Pause again.

IAN I didn't get to chat to you much last Friday.

JEAN No, no, I left soon after we got there.

IAN Yeah, I noticed.

JEAN It's kind of strange, seeing all those boys together.

IAN Men, now.

JEAN Yeah, some of them, anyway.

IAN They're a close group.

JEAN They are. It's good for Gary, I suppose, to have them.

IAN Yeah, yeah...poor old Gary.

JEAN Yeah...

Pause.

IAN So good weekend?

JEAN Great weekend! Well, it was quiet. But good. And you?

IAN Quiet, yeah. Working mostly.

JEAN At the weekends?

IAN It's a bit of tense time for the company.

JEAN I don't envy you.

IAN   Everyone seems to be saying that recently. Listen, it's a
job, I can't complain!

JEAN   I admire your attitude. What's your place like? You must
have the pick of the bunch.

IAN   Not really. We had to sell our family house after we went
bust back in...all that. So, my parents moved back into my
apartment.

JEAN   Wow. That's very good of you.

IAN   Well, they did technically own the apartment, so...

JEAN   Right...

IAN   And how's it all going moving back? Has much changed?

JEAN   God, no, everything's exactly the same...except for my
mother being...

IAN   Yeah. Course. Sorry.

JEAN   No, no.

IAN   You looking for a new job?

JEAN   No, I'm staying where I am. I can sort of work from
anywhere, which is handy. I'm looking after the statistics
and data analysis for this tech start-up firm.

IAN   Right, cool.

JEAN   Yes, people's eyes do seem to glaze over when I describe it.

IAN   No, I didn't mean to—

JEAN   I'm joking, you're fine. It's actually not as boring as it
sounds.

IAN   No, I'm sure.

JEAN   But I might look for something new once we're settled
in. It would be nice to meet some new people.

IAN   Totally. I even feel that. It's the same old people rattling
around here.

JEAN   We should get a drink sometime? If you fancied it?

A hesitation.

IAN Yeah. That would be nice. Although I don't know how Gary would feel if we...

JEAN I meant as friends.

IAN That's what I meant too! Friends. Obviously.

JEAN Obviously!

IAN Well, that's sorted then, let's do it, do that...sometime.

JEAN Let's!

Pause.

Although I would be flattered. Don't get me wrong!

IAN Well, me too. I haven't had a date in... I actually can't remember.

JEAN What? No way. Why is that?

IAN I don't know.

JEAN What's wrong with you?

IAN You tell me. It's not for lack of trying!

JEAN Maybe it's just that there's the same old people rattling around.

IAN Yes, that. Or it could be my palpable desire to be loved...

JEAN *laughs at this.*

GARY *enters the room.*

GARY Wasn't sure if it was twenty-eight or twenty-nine. Ooh, groovy carpet!

IAN Here he is, the man of international mystery!

GARY What's that supposed to mean?

IAN Nothing, we were just talking before you came in.

GARY About what?

JEAN   It was a stupid joke.

GARY   About me?

JEAN   No. We were speculating where you might be.

GARY   Why do you care?

JEAN   I don't. You were just being vague and mysterious, is all.

GARY   I don't need to tell you my every move. You're not my...

JEAN   I was joking, Gar, sorry. You're right, I absolutely don't need /to know.

GARY   If you must know, I go to see this woman, Miriam, every Monday at one. To talk about stuff.

IAN   That's great, man.

JEAN   Yeah, good for you, Gar.

GARY   See, this is why I shouldn't have said anything. Stop looking at me like that.

JEAN   Like what?

GARY   I can see you pitying me.

JEAN   I don't pity you? Actually, I'm looking at your ear piercing. It's really red.

GARY   It's grand!

JEAN   Are you sure? It's quite inflamed.

GARY   *(almost hissing)* Yes, I'm fuckin' sure. Stop judging me with your eyes.

JEAN   Alright, I'll look somewhere else!

GARY   It's not a big deal, seeing a therapist. It's actually really good for you, for your head, like.

JEAN   Gary, no one said it was a big deal?

GARY   You're acting as if it is.

JEAN   How am I acting like that?

GARY I don't want to talk about it anymore, alright?

JEAN Perfect.

GARY And don't be telling everyone that, right?

IAN No, not a big deal.

JEAN Who would I even tell?

GARY So what's the story with this place? Did you have a look around or what?

JEAN Not yet.

IAN Allow me.

> IAN *can start walking around the space as the other two observe it. A kind of tour.*

This place has been reduced in the last month so now would be a good time to snatch it. If the shoe fits, of course.

GARY Why's it been reduced?

IAN Well, it's been on the market a long time...

JEAN I'm sensing alarm bells here. Why's that?

IAN Let's just say there's a bit of work to do on the kitchen. But honestly, it's nothing that couldn't be fixed in a few months. And if the price is lower you might have a bit of wriggle room to do it up before you moved in.

JEAN What kind of work?

IAN Well, the bad news is... slugs. Under the floorboards. The wood is rotten.

JEAN Ugh.

GARY And the good news?

IAN They only come out at night. Most of the time.

JEAN Most of the time?

IAN Or wet weather.

GARY Which we don't get here... (GARY *secretly enjoys his own joke.*)

IAN Yeah, it's not ideal. But the location. I mean, talk about "up and coming"!

GARY Actually, my mate owns the coffee place around the corner.

JEAN Well, then! Where do we sign?

GARY It's more of a coffee van at the moment, but it will be a shop soon.

JEAN Great, that should increase the value of the house.

GARY I can't tell anymore if you're being sarcastic or not. It's actually a really nice van.

JEAN The coffee here is nothing compared to the coffee in Berlin.

IAN Really?

GARY That isn't true.

IAN I've always wanted to go there.

JEAN You should! I'll send you an email I give to everyone with lists of places to eat.

IAN That would be great.

GARY You're not going to Berlin, Ian.

IAN Why not?

JEAN Why wouldn't he?

GARY He's just saying that to impress you.

IAN I... No, I'm not.

JEAN Everyone wants to go there, it's a great city.

GARY It's just not very...Ian. I can't imagine you going there.

IAN Have you been?

GARY No.

IAN He never came to visit you while you lived there?

JEAN I know. Awful.

GARY You didn't want me to?

JEAN Yes, I did.

GARY Well, you could have told me that.

JEAN And you would have come?

GARY Maybe.

IAN Here, we could all go together? Or with the lads?

GARY I think we're spending enough time together as it is, Ian, don't you?

IAN Well, on that note, will I leave you two to have a look around?

JEAN How many more today?

IAN Just the two. And I've a good feeling about the next one!

GARY You say that every time, it's starting to get old now.

IAN *(He looks to* JEAN *for reassurance.)* Positivity gets you / everywhere.

JEAN No, it is starting to get a bit old, Ian.

IAN Noted.

7b.

28 Crescent Court

The following day, afternoon.

IAN is showing LAURA the same house from the previous scene.

LAURA is lying back on a reclining chair. IAN is behind her so she can't see he has his head in his hands.

LAURA A red front door. With a brass knocker in the shape of a... pine cone. Window boxes. Double-glazed panes on old frames. A belfast sink, yes, in the downstairs toilet *and* the kitchen. Two sinks. A free-standing bath! An Aga, like my grandmother had. A copper kettle... An ottoman! A winding staircase... A bay window.

Silence.

This one isn't for me.

IAN looks up.

IAN Laura. This is the third time I've shown you this place.

LAURA Is that a problem?

IAN No... I'm just saying...is there a reason for that? There must something drawing you back?

LAURA The lack of other options maybe?

IAN The location?

LAURA Desperation?

IAN It's a good investment.

LAURA Christ, if you use that word one more time. I'm not looking to invest my money, Ian, I'm looking to spend it. I just want a place to live in now. I want a home.

Her face crumples. IAN *does not know what to do.*

She regains composure surprisingly quickly. IAN *is relieved.*

I can't keep living with them, Ian. I just can't.

IAN I understand, trust me. I do.

LAURA My boyfriend is visiting this weekend. We're doing long-distance.

IAN Look, nothing worthwhile is ever easy, is it?

LAURA You've used that line before.

IAN Well, it's true!

LAURA I have to get home, Da has the dinner on.

IAN Trust me, the place I'm showing you tomorrow is a winner.

LAURA It better be, Ian.

IAN I've got a good feeling!

LAURA *just blankly looks at him. She's heard that line before too...*

8.

52 Marsala Road

Another few days later.

JEAN, IAN and GARY are looking around this small house. At this point, they are a bit jaded from the search.

JEAN I adored that last place. I can't believe it!

GARY I know you did.

JEAN Did you not?

GARY It was...fine.

JEAN Come on, it was miles better than anything else we've seen.

GARY It just didn't feel like...home.

JEAN None of them will feel like that immediately.

GARY I know that.

A silence. They look around the room they are in now.

JEAN This one...

GARY Yeah...

JEAN Not right.

GARY I don't mind it.

JEAN Gary, seriously? You didn't like the last place, but the fire stains on the wall here feel homely, do they?

GARY I can't help my taste!

JEAN I think you're just disagreeing with me on purpose.

GARY Why would I do that?

JEAN You tell me.

IAN *enters after being on the phone in another room.*

IAN "When the phone doth ring, thou shalt answer".

JEAN *gives a half smile,* GARY *ignores him.*

The eleventh commandment... So, what are we thinking?

GARY I like this one. Jean doesn't.

JEAN I much preferred the last place.

IAN Cuthbert Road.

JEAN And I liked that we were the first to view it, that felt special.

IAN Don't say I don't look out for you.

GARY There must be something wrong with it?

IAN Nothing, as far as I know.

GARY Honestly?

IAN Alright, full disclosure... It's haunted.

GARY What?

JEAN Gary's face!

GARY Are you serious?

IAN No!

JEAN He's obviously not. I absolutely adored the ceiling.

IAN I did think it had a European-y vibe to it, alright.

JEAN I was thinking that!

IAN Cultured.

GARY A cultured ceiling? Really, Ian?

JEAN My friend's apartment in Berlin had a slant in the ceiling just like that one. And she was a Swedish architect so obviously had excellent taste.

GARY Oh my God, again with the Berlin stuff. We get it okay? You're very multicultural. Everything here is completely crap compared to there. We know.

JEAN Well...yeah, it is.

GARY Why don't you just go back there then?

JEAN *Schoen wärs.*

GARY What did you say?

JEAN Nothing.

GARY What's the German for you're a fuckin' pretentious arsehole?

JEAN *Ich bin ein grosskotziges Arschloch und ich bin stolz drauf.*

GARY Well, I've no idea now if that's right or not.

IAN I'd say it is.

GARY No shit, Ian!

IAN Okay, let's all take a breath.

IAN *leads them in a deep breath in...and deep breath out.*

If I were you two, I would seriously be considering the last place. And I know I don't need to say it again, but the location is dreamy. Plus, it's the best you're going to get for your budget. That is a highly sought-after area these days.

JEAN And that'll be good if we want to sell it on later.

IAN Now you're talking! Absolutely.

GARY Hang on a second. Sell it on? We haven't even bought somewhere yet.

JEAN I'm talking a few years down the line here.

GARY   But I thought the plan was that we were going to look for a proper *home*, home like Mam wanted. Somewhere we can live in forever?

JEAN   Of course, and we are doing that, but who knows what'll happen in the next few years. I mean, the world is our oyster!

GARY   I don't like oysters.

JEAN   Have you ever tried them?

GARY   No. I just know I wouldn't like them.

JEAN   Look, let's not look into the future now. I'm only saying, it's a good thing the area is improving. That's the whole point of investing in property, you want the price of your house to go up. *(looks to* IAN*)* Isn't it?

IAN *gives her thumbs up.*

GARY   I thought the whole point was that I'd be happier somewhere new?

JEAN   Well, that too. But it's also a good investment of the money she left. And who knows what we'll want in a few years, maybe we'll want to move to the countryside, or you might get married and have ten kids.

GARY   This is all moving very quickly.

JEAN   Or we might want a bigger house? And then we could sell that place on for, I'm going to dream big here and say... double the price! We'd be rich!

GARY   That makes me feel like I'd be doing something wrong.

IAN   You've essentially just described my job.

JEAN   See? It's normal. That's property, baby!

GARY   You're starting to sound like him now.

IAN   No offence taken.

GARY I just want to find a home. A place I'm happy to stay in forever, especially if we're going to be spending all the money she left. I want to be sure.

JEAN I understand that, and that is absolutely the main plan, but I think you need to focus more on the potential each place has. Like Cuthbert Road! Come on Gary, it was perfect.

GARY I'm not sure...

JEAN What didn't you like about it?

GARY There was a little bit of mould in the corner of the kitchen.

JEAN There's mould in our house too. Plenty of it.

GARY Yeah but it's our mould.

JEAN Gary, listen, mould is mould, wherever it came from is irrelevant, I can't believe I'm having this argument. Ian, do you mind if we...have a second?

IAN Sure.

He doesn't move.

JEAN Alone.

IAN Great, I'll make a...

IAN *gives a vague phone gesture and leaves them alone.*

JEAN What's going on?

GARY What do you mean?

JEAN Why are you being like this?

GARY Like what?

JEAN Like being angry at me every time I open my mouth. Disagreeing with me for the sake of it.

GARY I'm not doing that?

JEAN *just waits for him to say more.*

I don't like you and Ian ganging up on me like that, as if I don't understand stuff.

JEAN We're not ganging up on you! Anyway, he's your friend. You know him better than me.

GARY Exactly. It feels weird that you're flirting with him.

JEAN Excuse me? I am not flirting with him?

GARY Why are you smiling then?

JEAN *(smiling)* I'm not smiling.

GARY All that gushing; "Oh, Ian, you have to go to Berlin, honestly, it's amazing blah, blah, blah."

JEAN I'm being polite! I've no interest in him, it's just a bit of banter. And keep your voice down, the walls are thin.

GARY He's just so annoying.

JEAN He's the nicest person I've met since I've got back.

GARY You just think that because he laughs at your jokes.

JEAN And what's the matter with that? Shouldn't I be making friends here?

GARY Yeah, just... Ian...

JEAN Look, I came back to be here for you. But I can't just be with you all the time.

GARY I don't want that either!

JEAN So then what's your problem?

GARY Nothing. I don't know. Can I just say one thing?

JEAN Please do.

GARY I would feel uncomfortable with you having relations with Ian.

JEAN "Having relations"... Wow, been a while, has it?

GARY You know what I mean.

JEAN Why would you feel uncomfortable about that?

GARY Because he's my friend and you're my sister.

JEAN That's all?

GARY What else would it be?

A pause. JEAN *regards him for a moment.*

JEAN Well, you don't need to worry about that.

GARY Fine. I'm not.

JEAN Good.

Silence.

GARY I hate this place.

JEAN I knew it. And the last place?

GARY I didn't like the horrible bin room out the front.

JEAN Every bin room is horrible! You're not going to find a comfortable bin room.

GARY I suppose.

JEAN I really liked it, Gary. I think it's the best we're going to get.

GARY Can I think about it?

IAN *comes back into the room.*

IAN Is the coast clear? What do you guys think of this one?

JEAN We like it. We really like it. Em...

GARY But we also hate it.

JEAN We really hate it.

IAN Fair enough! Pebble-dash is not for everyone.

JEAN But Cuthbert Road is staying in my head.

IAN Good choice! And right on your budget. It's going up on the website tomorrow morning so I can fend people off until you let me know. Although that patio out the back is going to be a huge attraction.

GARY *(suddenly interested)* That was a patio?

IAN What else would it be?

GARY I just thought it was a...space.

JEAN Yeah, we could grow plants, Gary. Or start a herb garden!

IAN Very good.

GARY A herb garden? Yeah...maybe.

9.

122 Gandon House

IAN *is standing catching his breath after walking up several flights of stairs, he is rambling on.*

LAURA *is busy on her phone, barely listening or looking at him.*

IAN We are talking *hundreds* of steps. It took a few hours, at least. But the view at the top was just...breathtaking. I was in much better shape at the time then...obviously.

And the people there...they are so...humble. It was incredible to experience such generosity, such genuinely kind people. Not like us, at all.

LAURA Mmm. Why are you talking about Japan?

IAN Because those stairs, kind of remind me of the climb I did on that trip. Weirdly!

LAURA *studies him for a moment...then quickly glances at the space around her.*

LAURA I don't like this place.

IAN Are you sure you don't want to have a proper look around first? You've just come all the way up here?

LAURA It's fine, it's good for my step count.

IAN Can I just say? Think about how you could "feng-shui" this place yourself. Perhaps a low coffee table here or a *futon*...maybe here?

LAURA You know my boyfriend is Korean, right?

IAN Yeah? I know... Why are you bringing that up?

He tries to lean on something. Then the buzzer for the door goes off. IAN, *saved by the bell, quickly turns away from* LAURA.

LAURA Are you expecting someone?

IAN I might have two other clients joining us. *(into intercom)* Fifth floor! Just about got my breath back...phew! So, like I said: it's highly in demand, very generous living space, all modern/ conveniences.

LAURA But what about the area? My friend was mugged in her own home last week.

IAN Does she live near here?

LAURA No, but still...people are doing that now. It's scary. Do you think I'd be safe here?

IAN Safe? Yes. You know sometimes I think...the more dangerous the area the more likely there is to be a police presence. So, in a way...you're safer to be here than say...somewhere that has absolutely no crime at all. People don't expect it there, you get me?

LAURA You're not making me feel great about it.

IAN There are three locks on the door. Working CCTV outside the building.

LAURA And the neighbours?

IAN Oh, they're murderers.

LAURA Ian.

IAN No, they are very nice people.

LAURA You've met all of them? Everyone in the building?

IAN The ones right below us, downstairs. I sold that flat to them.

LAURA I just find it strange to be sharing a building with so many strangers. Have you ever thought about that?

IAN That's city living! Maybe you should try the country side if that's a worry?

LAURA I'd definitely be murdered there. Too isolated.

IAN Why don't you have a look at the bedrooms?

As LAURA *goes to have a look,* IAN *turns away, he is running out of patience today. He takes a deep breath and starts to do a mindfulness technique.* JEAN *enters.*

JEAN Hello!

IAN Jean! Good to see you.

JEAN You too. Stressful day?

IAN The usual. *(slightly whispering)* I have another client in the bedroom.

JEAN Ah. Going okay?

IAN It's going... *(He gives a "who knows" gesture.)*

JEAN I came up the stairs two at a time. The lift is broken.

IAN I know...bad start. But there's a view. I give you a window!

JEAN Wow. So, this is what you meant by "panoramic views"?

IAN Did I say that?

JEAN It's on the website.

IAN Hmm, must take that down.

LAURA *comes back in.*

LAURA Oh, you've found the window, I see.

JEAN A coveted window!

LAURA Pity the view is...

IAN The sun sets...every evening. Somewhere. Sometimes you can catch it just in that corner.

JEAN Stunning.

LAURA I'm getting a crick in my neck already.

Suddenly the buzzer on the door starts going. It doesn't stop. It's persistent.

IAN Would that be...?

JEAN Just leave him.

IAN It's Gary, right? I'll tell him to come up.

JEAN Yeah, you don't have to let him in. I'm probably going to head now anyway.

IAN I'll go find him.

IAN exits. JEAN keeps glancing towards the door during the next exchange.

LAURA So... How long have you been looking around for?

JEAN About two weeks now.

LAURA Seen anything close to what you want?

JEAN Nearly...

LAURA It's hard, isn't it?

JEAN Tiring. How long have you been...?

LAURA Around three months. Ian's been patient, in fairness to him.

JEAN He really is, isn't he?

LAURA So, have you found somewhere?

JEAN I have a place in mind, yeah.

LAURA That's so great. Where is it?

JEAN Eh, I feel like I can't really say until we know. You know?

LAURA Of course, sorry.

Slight pause.

I mean we're probably looking for very different things anyway. Is it the one above the fire station?

JEAN No.

LAURA I've been back to see that one twice. It's starting to look tempting.

JEAN You don't sound enthused?

LAURA I'm not. But I'm desperate to like somewhere.

JEAN I can't believe how bad the market is since I came back.

LAURA Oh, where were you?

JEAN I just moved back from Germany.

LAURA Wow.

JEAN I was there for eight years.

LAURA What made you choose to live there?

JEAN Eh... It's such a long time ago. Actually, I saw it in a music video. And I thought...that's where I want to go. It seemed liberal and yet organised. And it was.

LAURA Nice to come back home though, isn't it? You'd miss the people?

JEAN Yeah. That's what everyone says. Nice people in Berlin too.

LAURA When I went travelling last year, I got really home sick.

JEAN Where were you?

LAURA Half way up to base camp in Nepal.

JEAN Whoops.

LAURA But it just hit me, like a wave of something. I just felt this pull towards...home. You know? I just missed it so much I had tears in my eyes and everything.

JEAN Right. Yeah.

LAURA Missed the air, or something. I could also have been running low on oxygen. Did you get that over there?

JEAN Not exactly...honestly, I never really thought about it.

LAURA Ireland is so different now than it was when you left, I'd say.

JEAN Only difference so far is that there's coffee shops everywhere!

LAURA I know, I love it. But, you know, the people are very liberal here now too.

JEAN Do you think so?

LAURA My cousin had a threesome last weekend.

Suddenly GARY *enters with a small bit of blood on his hand.* IAN *follows behind.*

GARY Well! You should have seen the look on his face. I fucking *(mimes punching someone)* I got him. He won't be shouting those kinds of things for a while. Scared shitless.

JEAN He was a teenage boy.

GARY So? He needs to know he can't be saying stuff like that around here anyway.

JEAN He wasn't older than sixteen I'd say.

GARY Jesus, you could say "thank you".

Beat.

What's wrong with you?

JEAN You're embarrassing me, that's what's wrong.

GARY Oh, I'm embarrassing you, really?

GARY *notices* LAURA.

How's it going?

LAURA Good.

IAN Laura, this is my—

LAURA Yes, we've met. Nice to...em.

GARY So, are we going to have a look around or what?

Nobody moves.

Right, fuck this.

IAN How about I...I'll show you out.

GARY Don't bother.

He goes to leave.

It wasn't my fault, it was his. You should be embarrassed about him, not me.

GARY *stalks out.*

IAN Sorry about that. Eh... Any questions about this place?

They don't really know what to say.

JEAN Nothing springs to mind.

IAN It's all on the website anyway. I really should make sure he gets out, that gate can be a tricky bastard. You two can have another look around if you like? The door locks when you close it behind you.

LAURA Great.

JEAN Thank you.

IAN All good!

IAN *leaves, giving a final double thumbs up.*

JEAN *and* LAURA *are alone again.*

JEAN Sorry about him...

LAURA You okay?

JEAN I'm fine... I don't know about him.

LAURA Men.

JEAN Men.

Pause.

LAURA So he's your...?

JEAN Brother.

LAURA Oh.

JEAN We're looking to buy a place together.

LAURA Right. But not to live in...

JEAN Together. Yes. He's hard work, though.

LAURA He'll grow out of it.

JEAN I've been waiting for that to happen for a long time... Do you have any siblings?

LAURA A sister.

JEAN Oh, that's—

LAURA We're not close.

JEAN Ah.

LAURA I can't imagine ever living with her again... Wouldn't do it to myself.

JEAN I'm starting to wonder that too...

LAURA Oh, no, you'll be fine! Sorry, I didn't mean...

JEAN No, of course. We'll be fine.

Silence for a moment.

LAURA Do you want to have another look around?

JEAN Not really.

LAURA Do you want to get a drink?

JEAN I would love that.

10.

98 Linton Avenue

A few hours later.

GARY *looking sheepish, is sitting in the living room. The boxes are still out.* **JEAN** *has just entered the room.*

GARY Where were you?

JEAN Just needed a bit of space.

A silence. **JEAN** *can take off her coat or settle into the room in a bit more.*

GARY Did you like that last apartment?

JEAN No.

GARY Me neither.

Back to silence. **JEAN**'s *not giving him anything.*

Did you go for a walk or something?

JEAN Yep.

GARY Where'd you go?

JEAN I don't need to tell you my every movement, do I?

Silence. Longer this time.

GARY You did my washing?

JEAN Yes.

GARY Thanks.

JEAN That was before you punched a child in my "honour".

GARY He wasn't a child! And it's not like I wanted to do that.

JEAN It seemed like you did?

GARY No one can get away with saying stuff like that anymore. Not here.

JEAN *just looks right through him.*

What? You can't just walk past and take that kind of shit now? Especially not from people like him.

JEAN "People like him".

GARY Yeah. You don't deserve that. No one does.

JEAN You know, when I left, that was you. You were the sixteen-year-old boy shouting abuse at people on the street. Unless you've just wiped that clean from your memory now?

GARY I wouldn't have said anything like that.

JEAN Well, you did and worse. I can remember that much.

GARY I haven't done anything like that for years.

JEAN But you used to?

GARY Yeah, I was a fuckin' eejit then! And it was just a bit of name-calling, innocent stuff, like. I didn't have a clue. I was a teenager.

JEAN Like that boy is now?

GARY You can't hold that shit against me. I'm very different to how I was back then. I've changed a lot.

JEAN You seem the same to me.

GARY I'm not the same! Jesus, you've no fucking clue who I am now.

JEAN Look at the blood on your hand, Gary.

GARY It's a graze!

JEAN I don't care what it is! You have this anger in you that's scary.

GARY You are making such a big deal out of this.

JEAN I don't want you to be like that.

GARY You can't decide what I'm like?

JEAN Do you talk to Miriam about this kind of thing?

GARY No? You are blowing this way out of proportion. I thought I was doing something nice for you. I want you to be safe. That's all.

JEAN I am safe. Are you? What do you talk to her about then?

GARY I don't want to go into it.

JEAN Do you talk about me?

GARY No?

JEAN About Mam? About our relationship?

GARY Hate to be the one who breaks this to you, but not everything revolves around you, did you know that?

JEAN It would be a normal thing to talk about. Isn't that what people basically go to therapy for? To recover from their family?

GARY I just talk about whatever has been happening that week. That's all. I'm not some closed-off fool who doesn't know his arse from his elbow, right? I talk about stuff. A lot. I just don't want to talk about it to *you*.

A pause. This stings.

JEAN Well, if you ever do...

GARY You don't need to worry about me.

JEAN You're making it hard...

GARY You didn't think about me for eight years. Why do you suddenly care now?

JEAN I did think about you. A lot.

GARY Didn't feel like it.

JEAN Why are you pushing me away here, Gary?

GARY I'm not!

JEAN You're making it difficult. It's not like you're spoiled for choice with people to care about you.

GARY I don't need anyone else.

JEAN We all need people. That's okay. I can admit I need people around me sometimes.

GARY Did you have people? In Berlin?

JEAN I did. Really great people.

GARY Better than me and Mam.

JEAN They were better for me at the time.

GARY I always wondered that; did you have a gang of friends other there.

JEAN I'm not some kind of loner, Gary! I had loads of friends, too many friends. I had to cut some because I couldn't keep up with them all.

GARY Did Mam meet any of them?

JEAN How would she have done that?

GARY When she was over?

JEAN Oh. No. She didn't.

GARY Right, probably not her sort.

JEAN No. We just spent the time together... You know, that teenager you hit. He needs people around him more than anyone.

GARY Look, I get it, I won't do it again, okay?

JEAN Good.

GARY And thanks for doing my washing.

JEAN Don't get too used to it.

GARY I found something when I was cleaning out my room.

JEAN If it's another cushion with a passive-aggressive slogan embroidered on it, I swear to God.

GARY It's even better.

JEAN What could possibly be better than that?

GARY *hands her a poorly wrapped Barbie-shaped object.*

JEAN *opens it carefully. It's Margaret. Her mermaid Barbie with a buzz cut and a demonic smile.*

Margaret... I knew she wouldn't have thrown her out.

GARY I still don't get why you liked her so much, but sure look...

JEAN You don't get this?

She flaunts Margaret in front of him again.

GARY She has a certain charm, I suppose.

JEAN I love her because Mam gave her to me even though she fought me over everything else... Margaret felt like a sort of triumph.

GARY You mean *Santa* gave her to you?

JEAN Yes, sorry, that was it. Of course, nothing was as straightforward in our family, had to be a bit of deceit somewhere...

GARY I think we should take that house, Jean.

JEAN What?

GARY The one with the nice ceiling.

JEAN Oh, Gary! Are you sure?

GARY Yeah. I think we should go for it.

JEAN Really?

GARY I think it's the right place for us.

JEAN Oh my God... Because I really don't think we'll find anywhere as nice.

GARY I know.

JEAN And I think it's actually quite good value for what we're paying. I mean, it's still high but it'll be a good investment, trust me.

GARY I know!

JEAN And compared to everything else we've seen it's basically a mansion. Compared to this place, even, it's almost as big!

GARY Jesus, I KNOW! I'm agreeing with you. It's my idea, you don't need to keep convincing me.

JEAN Sorry, sorry! Just saying, it's a good...

GARY *glares at her.*

It's a good decision.

GARY That's why I'm making it.

JEAN Thank you.

An awkward moment. GARY *feels strange about being amenable.*

GARY You're welcome.

JEAN So... This is exciting, right? You're happy?

GARY It's what she would have wanted. So, yeah.

JEAN Good. Good! Me too.

GARY I think it's funny, you know? How she's still dictating my life even while she's gone. Miriam pointed that out to me the other day.

JEAN Interesting idea from Miriam...

GARY But, I was saying to her, that's because she always wanted me to be happy. Even when the things she did might not have seemed that way, so I suppose, that's why I keep thinking about what she... *(He struggles to articulate his own thoughts.)* What I'm saying is, I think she would be happy we're buying this new place.

JEAN I'm glad you think so.

GARY So, will we tell Ian?

JEAN Yeah, I'd like to see it one more time first.

11.

19 Cuthbert Road

The following day.

JEAN *and* IAN *are looking around 19 Cuthbert Road.*
IAN *is attempting to open a bottle of Prosecco.*

JEAN Nineteen Cuthbert Road. *Nineteen* Cuthbert Road. I can really hear it, can't you?

IAN Rolls off the tongue.

JEAN Jean and Gary O'Donoghue at Nineteen *Cuth*bert Road. Christmas Drinks! At Nineteen Cuthbert Road. Engagement party! At Nineteen Cuthbert Road... I have a good feeling about this.

IAN Me too. I think it suits you!

She clocks IAN *struggling with the bottle.*

JEAN Is it bad luck to celebrate before we've put down an official offer?

IAN Eh... I can put this back?

A beat.

JEAN I've never been very superstitious!

IAN Good answer!

JEAN And look at this!

JEAN *rushes over to an object in the space.*

It's so... Does this come with it?

IAN ...Yes. Why not!

JEAN And the shower is definitely electric, right?

IAN That's right.

JEAN Always good. The patio isn't as big as I remembered. That's weird, isn't it? In my mind it was wider.

IAN You could still grow a healthy herb garden in it?

JEAN True.

IAN And it's big for this close to town. Two chairs. A small table. A bottle of white. What more do you need?

JEAN Is it south facing?

IAN I was afraid you'd ask me that.

JEAN So, no?

IAN No. But with the height of the back wall you wouldn't be getting much sun anyway...if that's any consolation.

JEAN Is that why the last tenants moved on?

IAN No, no, I don't think so.

JEAN Do you know what the neighbours are like?

IAN Can't say I do. But there was never any trouble as far as I know.

JEAN I just can't believe we've actually managed to agree on a place. I want to seal the deal before Gary changes his mind.

IAN Sounds good to me! The boss will be delighted I've managed to lock down a deal. Not that that should influence your decision-making... It's up to you, of course!

JEAN I think we're going to aim for just under the asking.

IAN Yes! My mother is hoping for that. And it just went on the market officially this morning so you're in good time.

JEAN Has there been anyone else in to see it?

IAN Few people coming later, but let's just say it's good you're getting the offer in early. We want to get it off our hands so I'll see what I can do about a speedy handover.

JEAN So the owners must be keen to sell it then?

IAN No, the company owns it. We were renting it until a few weeks ago.

JEAN Ah, so our fate is really in your hands. Well, fingers crossed!

IAN Like I said, I'll put in a good word.

He can wink at her here. He's loving having this influence.

JEAN Thank you, Ian. I don't know what we'd do without you, really.

She touches his shoulder or arm.

IAN It's a great deal, honestly. One of those situations where it was more expensive to rent it per month than it is to pay the mortgage. As long you have the deposit of course, like yourselves.

JEAN Oh God, *more* expensive than the mortgage? What's wrong with landlords?

IAN In fairness, that can't really be helped, it's the market. Sort of a catch twenty-two.

JEAN Is that really true? What if people in charge stopped raising the prices, maybe "the market" would drop? Or you could introduce rent caps? Like Berlin.

IAN Maybe. But how do you stop everyone else from raising them?

JEAN I don't know, round them all up, have a meeting, and... appeal to their humanity?

IAN That's funny.

JEAN What?

IAN You still believe in landlords' "humanity".

JEAN Or couldn't you just decide to do it in your company? Maybe other people would copy you?

IAN That's even more idealistic than your last idea.

JEAN I'm worse than an idealist, I'm a romanticist.

IAN Really? I wouldn't have pinned you as one.

JEAN Don't be fooled by my hard exterior. I'm already imagining you on the front page of the newspaper dragging down the property market, "the hero of affordable living".

IAN I think you've overestimated my sway in the company there. I don't get to make those kinds of calls. And I absolutely wouldn't be allowed on the newspaper... If I did make the decisions, I'd definitely give you this place for free!

JEAN offers a half-hearted smile.

Or at least at a heavily subsidised rate.

JEAN God. How did the last tenant afford it?

A moment.

IAN He didn't really.

JEAN So that's why he left.

IAN Yeah... He actually... It's not a very nice story.

JEAN Why?

IAN Well, he wasn't paying his rent on time. And we had to keep raising it to keep up with the area. That's just the business, you know, that's how things work.

JEAN Sure.

IAN I don't know why I'm telling you this...

JEAN doesn't say anything but allows a silence, so he decides to continue.

He was three payments behind, so I was sent over to find him and tell him that he had to pay up or leave and then I found him...over there.

JEAN Found him as in...

IAN Found him...yeah. He had used a bed sheet.

JEAN Christ.

IAN It was really, really awful. He didn't have any family in the country, I think, because after the ambulance got here, I had to take his phone and call through his most recent numbers. And I was just listening to a foreign dial tone for a while until no one answered...

JEAN Jesus, Ian.

IAN And then after I left, I never found out if anyone eventually did answer. And a few weeks later, we hired people to clean it all out. So, the next time I came in here it was just like this. Like nothing had happened at all.

JEAN Do you think he did it because he couldn't pay the rent?

IAN We don't know. You can't really blame yourself for these things, my mother has said. People will decide to do something because they think there's no way out and you'll never really know why. I thought I would never be able to stop thinking about it. After seeing him like that. But actually... *(a shift in atmosphere)* it's funny how quickly we move on, isn't it? I suppose it's easier that way. Your brain just allows you to forget some things that are too painful to remember. Now it seems like a totally different place. I'll hand it to the redecorators, they really did a great job.

JEAN Did he seem off? Had he seemed in danger before you raised the rent?

IAN In danger from what?

JEAN Were there signs he might do something like that?

IAN I don't know, I never met him. We don't tend to discuss things with the tenants, we just send them a letter saying the rent is going up. That's how we do it, anyway. Easier.

JEAN Right. No human contact so no one can feel guilty?

IAN I do feel guilty. That's why I'm telling you now. Sorry, is this making you feel..?

JEAN No. No, it's good to know.

IAN It's more common than you think. Hard to find a property nowadays without a past. I didn't want to say anything in front of Gary, you know, people like him can feel strange about buying places after... Superstitious, like. But I wanted to be honest with you, as a friend. Not an agent.

JEAN And do you feel strange about selling it? As an agent?

IAN A part of me does. Another part of me thinks it's a good house in a nice area. If someone can afford it, happy days for everyone involved. Win-win.

JEAN "Win-win" for everyone except the man who couldn't afford it...

IAN His name was Simon. I think it was Simon. I think that's what it said on the form.

They can be sitting close together by now.

They both stare at the spot that **IAN** *had pointed out earlier.*

Suddenly **IAN** *turns to* **JEAN** *and kisses her.* **JEAN** *pulls away immediately after her brain gets over the shock.*

You okay?

JEAN Yeah.

IAN *goes in for the kill again,* **JEAN** *dodges him this time.*

Ian...

IAN Thank you for listening to me.

JEAN That's fine.

IAN It's been so nice to have someone to talk to about... everything.

JEAN Of course.

IAN *kisses her again, she is frozen.*

IAN What's wrong?

JEAN Look, I don't think this is...

IAN Stop worrying about Gary.

JEAN It's not him.

He is very close to her.

IAN Then what?

JEAN Can you just give me some space?

He moves away a bit.

IAN Why are you suddenly being so weird?

JEAN I'm not.

IAN You're acting as if I'm some kind of freak, all of a sudden.

JEAN Look, I'm sorry. I don't find you attractive...in that way.

IAN What was all that about then?

JEAN All what about?

IAN All the flirting, all the arm-touching, all the sucking up to me.

JEAN I like you as a friend, Ian. I never meant to...

IAN Lead me on? Right, you've found your house now, so the act is dropped.

JEAN There's no act. I don't want to kiss you, be man enough to take that on the chin.

He grabs her arm a bit too tightly.

IAN Well, it's a bit difficult when you're saying one thing one minute and another the next. Bit hard to keep up, like.

JEAN I never meant to offend you, I really didn't—

IAN Well, you are offending me. YOU ARE.

JEAN Ian, please...

He lets go of her.

IAN Jesus. I thought you were different, turns out you're a cunt like all the rest of them.

LAURA *enters.*

LAURA Ian? Oh. You've company.

JEAN *is relieved there is another person in the room.*

JEAN Hi! Laura.

LAURA You're after this place too?

IAN She doesn't like it. Out of her price range.

JEAN /Ian?

LAURA Oh, that's unfortunate.

IAN Yeah, it is.

LAURA Pity, this is by far the nicest place I've seen yet. It just came on the market this morning, I believe. Early birds!

JEAN Someone died in here.

LAURA What?

A silence. JEAN *and* IAN *aren't looking at each other.*

You know, I had a strange feeling when I came in here, I thought the atmosphere was...there was something off.

JEAN And we're going with another agent, anyway.

LAURA Oh?

LAURA *looks to* IAN *but he isn't meeting her eyes either.*

JEAN But best of luck with the rest of your search.

LAURA Yes. You too.

JEAN Right.

JEAN *leaves, no acknowledgement to* IAN. *A silence.*

LAURA Well?

IAN What?

LAURA You going to say anything here?

IAN What do you want me to say?

LAURA Maybe "Sorry, Laura"? "Sorry for wasting your time... again".

IAN I'm not going to say that. It's a nice house.

LAURA Maybe "Sorry, Laura, you deserve better than this"?

IAN What makes you think that?

LAURA Excuse me?

IAN What makes you think you deserve better than this?

LAURA *is thrown by him saying this to her.*

LAURA Eh... I...

IAN Was it your upbringing? Your childhood?

LAURA How dare you. How dare you assume things about me—

IAN You don't "deserve" anything. Whoever told you that you did, whoever put that thought in your tiny head, was wrong. Because none of us do.

LAURA I don't need to listen to this from you. And I don't need you to be wasting my time anymore than you already have.

IAN Good. Go with someone else then, see if they can rustle up anything to your standards, good luck to them.

LAURA I was giving you a big chance here, Ian. You blew it.

LAURA *goes to exit but before she goes (this is more to the house than to* IAN*) –.*

Pity. I might have liked this place. Nice ceiling.

She leaves. IAN *is alone.*

He puts his head in his hands. He gets up. His phone rings. He silences it. He looks at the spot where Simon died. He kicks something over...shouts.

12.

98 Linton Avenue

A few hours later. **GARY** *is observing* **JEAN**, *who is holding Margaret on the couch.*

GARY What's wrong with you?

JEAN Nothing.

GARY You sure? You've been quiet all day.

JEAN Yeah.

GARY I don't think it's that big of a deal.

JEAN No?

GARY No. We'll find another place we both like, you'll see.

JEAN Yeah. Definitely.

GARY Did Ian say why they took it off the market?

JEAN No.

GARY Were you talking to him at all?

JEAN Just briefly.

GARY You hold her when you're upset, you know.

JEAN Do I?

GARY Yeah. I've noticed.

JEAN Oh.

She regards Margaret and puts her down casually. **GARY** *picks her up.*

GARY Why Margaret?

JEAN Em... Well, I suppose, it felt like a kind of triumph when Mam—

GARY No, why the name "Margaret"? It's so granny-ish.

JEAN She was a girl in the class above me. She had long blonde hair...she was perfect.

GARY You wanted to be her?

JEAN I think everyone did.

GARY Wait, not Margaret O'Shea?

JEAN Yes!

GARY She's living down the road. Her brother was in my class.

JEAN I wonder, does she rock a buzz cut now too?

GARY Or maybe a fishtail.

He makes Margaret swim in the air.

JEAN I'm still annoyed you did that.

GARY What?

JEAN Cut off all Margaret's hair. That was a really evil thing to do.

GARY I was five years old.

JEAN You were eight. And I was devastated.

GARY I was max seven.

JEAN You were so cruel to me back then.

GARY Jesus, Jean. How many times do I need say I'm sorry? I feel like I'm constantly stepping on eggshells around you. Can't even ask a bloody question or I'm chained to the cross again.

JEAN You don't like being reminded of what you were like then.

GARY No! I've no problem with that, I've accepted it, I just don't see the point in lugging it all back up again and again. I don't think you've accepted I've changed now, I'm not going around cutting Barbie's hair off anymore.

JEAN Promise?

GARY I'm being serious, you know what I mean. I've grown up. I'm not just your little brother anymore, I'm a whole different person if you'd just let yourself get to know me. You're allowed change, right? Ian's allowed change. Everybody's allowed to change, except me, it seems. In your head I'm just...a thug who shouts names and beats people up.

JEAN *just looks at him.*

It's annoying.

JEAN What do you mean "Ian's allowed change"?

GARY Well, you know...all that stuff with Anna Murphy... And look at him now; he has a great job, everyone's giving him a second chance, no bother on him!

JEAN What stuff?

GARY Ah come on. The stuff that came out during my last year of school?

JEAN I wasn't here then.

GARY You must have heard about it.

JEAN Heard what?

GARY Are you serious? Mam must have told you this.

JEAN I don't know what you're on about.

GARY It was in the news.

JEAN What was?

A pause.

GARY It's not really my place to be telling you his business.

JEAN You just said it was in the news.

GARY Some news. Local papers. I don't know about others...

JEAN Just tell me then.

GARY He... I really thought you knew this? There were accusations made against him.

JEAN About what?

GARY About something he may or may not have done...

JEAN To who?

GARY Anna. A girl in our year. They made Ian leave school and everything, he finished the year from home. There was going to be a trial but the charges were dropped.

JEAN How come?

GARY Don't know. There were a few rumours flying around that she was worried about proving it. I don't know, she might have just wanted to get on with her life. But, one of the lads, whose father works with Anna's father, said Ian's Mam paid for her whole university education. Found her a flat and everything... that's why they moved out of their massive gaff. But I don't know, that could just be a rumour.

Puts his hands up as if to say; "you tell me what that means".

JEAN So you think she made it up to get free tuition?

GARY No! I'm not implying anything, I'm telling you the information I have. You can decide what to think or not.

JEAN And where is she now? The girl.

GARY I think she's in America. I never really saw her again after school, none of us did.

JEAN Do you think he did something?

GARY No. Come on. Ian, like? He's just an idiot and she was... Look, even if he did do it, after all that mess, he's not going to ever do it again, is he?

JEAN How do you know that?

GARY Because his life was runied.

JEAN *His* life?

GARY No one spoke to him for about five years after that even though nothing was proven. Plus, I would literally kick the living shit out him if I heard he had done something like that again.

JEAN Would you?

GARY Yes! And don't go on at me about not beating people up because this is a different thing, people deserve it for stuff like that. Sick, like.

JEAN Do you think his clients know?

GARY I don't know.

JEAN Shouldn't they be told?

GARY Again, it wasn't a proven guilty type of thing, it was all rumours and hush-hush so why should they?

JEAN You let me go there on my own today.

GARY Yeah, so?

JEAN Knowing he's been accused of doing something like that...

GARY Ah, Jean. Come on. You've been on your own with him loads before. Anyway, this is what I'm saying, even if he did do something, shouldn't he be allowed to grow up. A second chance. He's not a bad guy, like.

JEAN But you just told me—

GARY And you're the one who goes on about not protecting you and letting you get on with things by yourself, aren't you?

JEAN I just don't understand why you didn't even think to mention it.

GARY Because it's in the past, it was years ago! I presumed you knew. Everyone knows! I don't know how you didn't.

A beat.

Did something happen today?

She hesitates.

JEAN No. I just wish you had told me.

GARY I thought maybe Mam would have told you when she went over.

JEAN Oh, Jesus, Gary.

GARY What's going on with you?

JEAN Why does no one talk about it anymore?

GARY People just move on to the next thing eventually, I suppose.

JEAN Just when I was starting to think the place might have changed. Threesomes and flat whites don't mean anything if what's underneath is still the same.

GARY What are you on about?

JEAN Look, I want to be honest with you.

GARY Good. .

JEAN But I'm worried about telling you...

GARY Why?

JEAN Because I don't want you to fly off the handle.

GARY Fucksake! What kind of person do you think I am?

JEAN Look at what you did literally a few days ago?

GARY That was different.

JEAN How?

GARY Because he was a stranger. You're my sister!

JEAN And you're still my little brother.

GARY Yes, because you haven't let me be anything else! You
need to trust me, you need to give me the chance to show
you I've changed. We are two adults now, I want to have
the kind of relationship where we can rely on each other,
were we can trust each other, let each other in. Don't you
want that too?

JEAN Of course, I do.

GARY You know you can tell me anything.

JEAN Can I?

GARY Yes. Give me the chance to be there for you.

JEAN Okay.

GARY What is it, Jean?

A beat.

JEAN I never met Mam in Berlin.

A pause. GARY *is knocked off course.*

GARY What?

JEAN I never met her.

GARY When?

JEAN When she came over to see me.

GARY But you told me she...?

JEAN I know. I'm sorry.

GARY So...what happened? Where did she go?

JEAN She did come to Berlin. And I saw her at the station
where we had arranged to meet. I was waiting across the
road and she was just standing there looking around for me.

GARY Did she see you?

JEAN No.

GARY Why didn't you go over to her?

JEAN I watched her for a while. She must have been melting in that heat. She was wearing a little scarf and a pair of black tights. Black tights! It was thirty something degrees.

GARY So what, you couldn't be seen with someone wearing tights?

JEAN No. No... I just didn't want her to see me. As me. I was afraid.

GARY Of course. It always comes back to you, what you feel.

JEAN Don't think for a second that I don't deeply regret what I did. I think she had gotten her hair done and everything.

GARY She did, yeah, especially. She said it would last all weekend.

A pause.

So, what did she do then? Where did she stay?

JEAN I don't know.

GARY What do you mean you don't know?

JEAN I turned off my phone.

GARY You turned off your phone? She had come all that way and you...you turned *off* your phone. So you didn't see her at all?

JEAN No, Gary, I just told you—

GARY Yeah, and I'm really trying here now to get my head around this but.... Did you want to talk to her?

JEAN No. Yes. I thought I did but then when I saw her... I was terrified.

GARY Of what?

JEAN Of everything. Of what she might say to me.

GARY She was making the effort to see you. She wanted to reach out. She was trying to.

JEAN And do you think it would have been like you imagined? All smiles and laughing, and her welcoming me back with open arms? Really?

GARY I don't know, she had eight years to figure it out. You never gave her the chance.

JEAN I know and I wish I had done it differently but I didn't. You cannot understand how it feels, okay? How scared I was at the time.

GARY Well, so was she, I bet. Spending a whole weekend in Berlin alone. I don't care how it feels for you, you can't just leave a woman in her sixties, who has barely been out of the country, alone in a huge terrifying city.

JEAN Berlin isn't that terrifying, Gary—

GARY Don't give me that! Don't patronise me, I know what a city is like, okay, I've travelled places too. Not on my own, mind... Fucksake. So, when she came back...she had just spent the whole weekend alone... Why did she lie to me?

JEAN I really don't know. That surprised me too. I thought it would be the first thing you said to me when I came back. I presumed you two would be bitching about me like crazy back here.

GARY Again, not everything is about you. You know, we actually didn't talk about you a lot. Maybe for the first year you were gone, yeah, we'd ask each other how we thought you were and then after that, after it became clear you weren't bothered or interested in us, we just...stopped. You didn't really come up that much.

JEAN Good to know you were thinking of me.

GARY Did you ever think of me? I doubt it.

A moment.

JEAN And what about after Berlin?

GARY I asked her how the trip was when I was driving her home and she said it was fun.

JEAN And that was it?

GARY "It was fun" ...What the fuck did she do? Did that ever cross your mind?

JEAN Of course, it did.

GARY You didn't think to ask, no? Check she got home okay?

JEAN *shakes her head, no.*

JEAN We didn't speak again after that.

GARY How long did she stand there, like a fool, waiting for you? How long did it take her to realise you weren't coming, ha?

JEAN I don't know.

It dawns on him.

GARY So, you never saw her before she died?

JEAN No.

GARY Fucking hell.

JEAN Gary, you have to understand—

GARY I am so sick of understanding!

GARY *suddenly grabs Margaret.*

JEAN What are you doing?

GARY I kept her for you. I saw Mam had put her in the bin, so I saved her and took her out again when she wasn't watching. I hid her in my room in case you ever came back.

JEAN Thank you, Gary that's so sweet of—

GARY *breaks off one of Margaret's arms.*

What are you doing? Stop!

He rips off the other one.

Gary, stop! Please. Gar, listen to me. Today, in the house viewing. Ian...he...he did something to me.

GARY *stops trying to rip off Margaret's tail.*

He kissed me and I tried to tell him to stop but it was... strange and he made me feel very uncomfortable.

GARY Jesus Christ. You're unbelievable.

JEAN What? You just said you want a relationship where we can be honest with each other, rely on each other, I'm trying to / tell you

GARY That was before I knew you were lying to me the whole time.

GARY *throws Margaret on the floor, stands up and starts pacing around.*

JEAN What's wrong with you?

GARY You have no shame, you know that?

JEAN What?

GARY I just find it incredible how you have absolutely no sense of obligation to anyone but yourself. It's fuckin' sickening how selfish you are.

JEAN Gary, if you would just listen to me—

GARY No, you listen to me. You have *always* been like that.

JEAN Because I've always had to! I was dying in this house alone with you and her. And you know what? I am happy I never saw her again. Because when I left, she was a bully and a bigot, and I am glad she's dead now.

GARY *grabs* JEAN *by the collar of her clothes.*

Oh, you're going to hit me, are you?

GARY Don't fucking make me.

JEAN *(spits it)* You're exactly the same as her.

GARY *hits her.*

A horrible silence. He immediately regrets what he has does. JEAN *holds her face.*

GARY Is that what you wanted?

Nothing.

I'm sorry.

Nothing.

Jean. I'm so sorry—

JEAN You can't help yourself, can you?

GARY I know you won't believe this, but I am only this person when I am around you.

A silence.

JEAN No... I don't believe that.

13.

98 Linton Avenue

A few weeks later.

GARY *is showing* **LAURA** *around their mother's house. All boxes are packed away.*

LAURA What are the neighbours like?

GARY There's an old couple on one side and an old lady on the other.

LAURA I see.

GARY She's grumpy, but the couple are... I don't really know them, but they seem nice.

LAURA How long have you lived here for?

GARY Just...my entire life!

LAURA And you don't know your neighbours?

GARY They keep to themselves. My Mam knew them better.

LAURA So, this is your family home?

GARY Yeah.

LAURA I feel bad now!

GARY No, no, don't. We're ready to sell.

LAURA Awh, that's so nice. So, all three of you lived here at one stage?

GARY Yep!

LAURA That sounds cramped.

GARY No. No, it was...cosy. But my mother she, eh, she passed away recently.

LAURA Yes, Jean mentioned that. Oh God, I feel awful now.

GARY No, no, please, it's grand.

LAURA *(whispered)* Did she die in here?

GARY No. In the hospital. Well, no, in the ambulance.

LAURA I'm so, so sorry.

GARY Honestly, don't worry about it.

LAURA So, does Jean still live here too?

GARY No, no, she lives in...she lives just down the road.

LAURA So we'd be neighbours if I lived here?

GARY It's kind of further down the road though, a few streets back, is what I meant.

LAURA That must be nice having her so close by.

GARY Yeah, it is...

LAURA And how are you doing? Are you...feeling better?

GARY Feeling great, yeah. Thanks. Do you want to have another look upstairs?

LAURA Of course, yes, sorry for prying.

GARY No, no, you weren't.

A pause, because she was prying. LAURA *distracts herself by looking around.*

LAURA The things you could do with this place, my imagination is whirring!

GARY Oh? Good!

LAURA I have to tell you, it seems really perfect for me.

GARY It's been a good house.

LAURA And what exactly is included in the sale?

GARY *wasn't prepared for this question.*

GARY Everything?

LAURA Really? The last place I viewed told me they were taking out the light fittings.

GARY I really mean everything. You can even have the furniture if you want?

LAURA Are you sure?

GARY Absolutely.

LAURA I'll probably throw it all out eventually, but it would be so useful to get started.

GARY Well, it's yours, if you want it.

LAURA So what's the catch here?

GARY There isn't one?

LAURA There must be something wrong with it?

GARY I'm trying to think of something wrong with it... Nothing that I know of?

LAURA Why are you leaving here if nothing's wrong?

GARY For a change of scene.

LAURA Ooh. Where are you moving on to?

GARY Think I'm going to go to Australia.

LAURA Wow, could you think of anywhere further away?

GARY Nope.

A beat. He has not taken this as the joke she intended it to be.

LAURA Good for you.

GARY Yeah, I'm excited. Bit of sun on the bones, new places to see... It'll be good!

LAURA Oh, the weather! I might think about following you over there!

She laughs and GARY *looks briefly alarmed.*

Your sister will miss you.

GARY Yeah...

LAURA I have to say, I am really, really excited about this place. It looks pretty close to perfect. Almost exactly what I'm looking for.

GARY Almost?

LAURA You know, you have this picture in your mind of what your future home will look like when you start the search, don't you?

GARY I know what you mean.

LAURA So then it's hard to find the exact one because...the picture you have doesn't exist! And it still won't exist until you live in it for a while and things become familiar. But I think this place could be the one. The one that becomes familiar... After some serious redecoration, of course.

GARY Of course.

LAURA Not that it's not... I love brown! But I want to start a family soon and things will need to be brighter then because—

GARY You don't have to explain, it's okay. It's old-fashioned, I know. We never got around to changing it...

LAURA No! It's homely. It's lived in!

GARY *just smiles. He's growing tired of this rigmarole.*

That chair is... I love it... Do you mind if I have another quick look upstairs?

GARY Please do.

LAURA *goes towards the stairs.* GARY *catches her before she's gone.*

Oh! Eh, the cold tap in the downstairs toilet. You have to really twist that to get the water to come out.

LAURA But the water still comes out, right?

GARY Like you have to twist it around at least twice and you think no water is coming out and then it does. So, that's a bit annoying.

LAURA Thanks for telling me. I think I could live with that.

GARY Yes, and the window in my mother's room? That one is very stiff. You need to kind of push against it and then pull.

He mimes this for her.

How I do it is: I push with my shoulder and then pull it up quickly. Push and pull. It gave me a splinter once but I'm sure that won't happen to you.

LAURA I was thinking I'd have new windows installed anyway, single glaze is very eighties. I'm just glad it has them!

GARY Cool. Yeah, probably a good shout.

LAURA I suppose that's the joy of buying an old house, it comes with its own quirks and surprises.

GARY Absolutely.

LAURA That's why it's so nice to meet the seller directly.

GARY Cut out the middle man.

LAURA Exactly. Cut him out. I couldn't trust that last guy I had.

GARY Oh, really?

LAURA Something about him I just didn't like... Couldn't put my finger on it.

A moment. GARY *doesn't know what to say to that.*

GARY Sure, have another look around, I'll be here if you have any questions.

LAURA Thanks, Gary. I won't be too long.

GARY No, please! Take all the time you need...

LAURA *goes off to look upstairs.*

GARY *walks over and sits down in his mother's chair. He waits a few moments for* LAURA *to come down again.*

Lights down.

The End

PROPS

A cushion with "home is where you hang your heart" stitched on it.
Margaret – a Mermaid Barbie with a buzz cut and a demonic smile.
Bottle of Prosecco, two plastic glasses they can drink it from.
Two beers.
An old game of Guess Who?

Furniture and props can be used at the designer's discretion in a preferably non-naturalistic way to create the surroundings of lots of the unloved and unused houses, flats and homes.

SOUND EFFECTS

Music should be used during the scene changes at the discretion of the director.

VISIT THE SAMUEL FRENCH BOOKSHOP AT THE ROYAL COURT THEATRE

Browse plays and theatre books, get expert advice and enjoy a coffee

Samuel French Bookshop
Royal Court Theatre
Sloane Square
London
SW1W 8AS
020 7565 5024

Shop from thousands of titles on our website

 samuelfrench.co.uk

 samuelfrenchltd

 samuel french uk